Tales from the

TERRIFIC REGISTER

⟹◈⟸

The Book of Ghosts

First published 1825
This edition first published 2010

The History Press
The Mill, Brimscombe Port
Stroud, Gloucestershire, GL5 2QG
www.thehistorypress.co.uk

British Library Cataloguing in Publication Data.
A catalogue record for this book is available from the British Library.

ISBN 978 0 7524 5416 0

Typesetting and origination by The History Press
Printed in India by Nutech Print Services

Tales from the

TERRIFIC REGISTER

The Book of Ghosts

EDITED BY
CATE LUDLOW

THE

TERRIFIC

REGISTER;

OR,

RECORD OF

Crimes, Judgments,

PROVIDENCES, AND CALAMITIES.

London:
PUBLISHED BY SHERWOOD, JONES, AND CO.
AND HUNTER, EDINBURGH.

1825.
Printed by T. Richardson, 98, High Holborn.

GOD'S REVENGE AGAINST MURDER

Editor's Note

The *Terrific Register* is part of the glorious, gruesome, sensational, shocking and downright dreadful underbelly of nineteenth-century publishing. The Victorians, who we love to picture as prudish, had an absolute mania for gore: they read papers with headlines such as 'Shocking Murder of a Wife with a Scythe!', bought hundreds of 'authentic' accounts of executions, and loved anything to do with dark deeds, adventure and the supernatural. This collection is one of the forerunners of the genre of penny bloods and dreadfuls, the epitome of this underbelly. The roots of this genre, roughly speaking, are simple: all at once printing was cheap, and everyone – including the very poorest children – could read. Children and adults, from the slums all the way upwards, wanted something exciting to thumb through. They got it in titles such as *Varney the Vampire, or, the Feast of Blood*; *History of the Pirates of All Nations*; *Sweeney Todd, The Demon Barber of Fleet Street*; *The Wild Boys of London* and so on.

All of these stories in the *Terrific Register* are (allegedly) true. Some of them are fairly surprising. None are pleasant. Whatever magazine or series of books you devoured as a child, rest assured that the child of 185 years ago felt the same about the *Terrific Register*. You won't find anything more gruesome, more hideous, more hair-raising or more downright fun to dip into.

The Book of Ghosts

Apparition Of The Duchess Of Mazarine, Mistress to Charles II, To Mad. De Beauclair, Mistress To James II

It is well known to most people acquainted with the English history, that the celebrated Duchess of Mazarine was mistress to King Charles II. Mr Waller particularly takes notice of her, as one of the favourites of that monarch.

7

Madame de Beauclair was a lady equally admired and beloved by his brother and successor, James II. Between these two ladies there was an uncommon friendship, such as is rarely found in persons bred up in courts; particularly those of the same sex, and in the same situation.

But the similarity of their circumstances might contribute a good deal towards it, they having both lost their royal lovers; the one by death, the other by abdication. They were both women of excellent understandings; had enjoyed all that the world could give them; and were arrived at an age in which they might be supposed to despise all its pompts and vanities. We shall, without any further introduction, give the whole of the revelation, in the author's own words; who declared himself to be an eye-witness of the truth of it.

After the burning of Whitehall, these two ladies were allotted very handsome apartments in the Stable-yard, St James; but, the face of public affairs being then wholly changed, and a new set of courtiers, as well as rules of behaviour, coming into vogue, they conversed almost only with each other.

About this time it was that reason first began to oppose itself to faith, or, at least, to set up against it by some, who had an ambition to be thought more penetrating than their neighbours. The doctrine soon spread, and was too much talked of not to be frequently a subject of conversation for these two ladies; and, though I cannot say that either of them were thoroughly convinced by it, yet the specious arguments made use of by persons of high reputation for learning, had such an effect on both, as to raise great doubts in them concerning the immateriality of the soul, and the certainty of its existence after death.

In one of the serious consultations they had together on this head, it was agreed between them that on which ever of them the lot should fall to be first called from this world, she should return, if there was a possibility of doing so, and give the other an account of in what manner she was disposed of. This promise it seems was often repeated, and the duchess happening to fall sick, and her life despaired of by all about her, Madame de Beauclair reminded her of what she expected from her; to which Her Grace replied, she might depend upon her performance. These words passed between them, not above an hour before the dissolution of that great lady, and were spoken before several persons who were in the room, but at that time they were far from comprehending the meaning of what they had said.

Some years after the duchess's decease, happening, in a visit I made to Madame de Beauclair, to fall on the topic of futurity, she expressed her disbelief of it with a great deal of warmth, which a little surprised me, as being of quite a contrary way of thinking myself, and had always, by the religion she professed, supposed her highly so. I took the liberty of offering some arguments, which I imagined would have been convincing to prove the reasonableness of depending on a life to come: to which she answered, that not all the whole world could say should ever persuade her to that opinion; and then related to me the contract made between her and her departed friend, the Duchess of Mazarine.

It was in vain I urged the strong probability there was that that souls in another world might not be permitted to perform the engagements they had entered into in this; especially when they were of a nature repugnant to the Divine Will. But nothing I could say made the least impression; and I found, to my great concern, that she was become as great an advocate for the new doctrine of non-existence after death as any of those who first proposed it; on which, from that time forward, I avoided all discourse with her on that head.

It was not, however, many months after we had this conversation, that I happened to be at the house of a person of condition, whom, since the death of the Duchess of Mazarine, Madame de Beauclair had the greatest intimacy with of any of her acquaintance. We were just sat down to cards about nine o'clock in the evening, as near as I can remember, when a servant came hastily into the room, and acquainted the lady I was with that Madame de Beauclair had sent to entreat she would come that moment to her; adding, that if she ever desired to see her more in this world, she must not delay her visit.

So odd a message might very well surprise the person to whom it was delivered; and, not knowing what to think of it, she asked who had brought it? And being told it was Madame de Beauclair's groom of the chamber, ordered he should come in, and demanded of him, if his lady were well, or if he knew of any thing extraordinary that had happened to her which should occasion this hasty summons. To which he answered, that he was entirely incapable of telling her the meaning; only as to his lady's health, he never saw nor heard her ladyship complain of the least indisposition.

'Well then,' said the lady, (a little out of humour,) 'I desire you'll make my excuse, as I have really a great cold, and am fearful the night air may increase it, but to-morrow I will not fail to wait on her very early in the morning.'

The man being gone we were beginning to form several conjectures on this message of Madame de Beauclair; but, before we had time to agree on what might be the most

10

feasible occasion, he returned again, and with him Mrs Ward, her woman, both seemingly very much confused and out of breath.

'O madam,' cried she, 'my lady expresses an infinite concern that you should refuse this request, which she says will be her last. She says that she is convinced of her not being in a condition to receive your visit to-morrow; but, as a token of her friendship, bequeaths you this little casket, containing her watch, necklace, and some jewels, which she desires you will wear in remembrance of her.'

These words were accompanied with the delivery of the legacy she mentioned, and that, as well as Mrs Ward's words, threw us both into a consternation we were not able to express. The lady would fain have entered into some discourse with Mrs Ward concerning the affair; but she evaded it by saying, she had only left an undermaid with Madame de Beauclair, and must return immediately; on which the lady cried all at once, 'I will go with you; there must be something very uncommon certainly in this.' I offered to attend her, being, as well I might, desirous of getting some light into what at present appeared so mysterious.

In fine, we went that instant; but, as no mention was made of me, nor Madame de Beauclair might not probably be informed I was with the lady when her servant came, good manners and decency obliged me to wait in a lower apartment, unless she gave leave for my admittance. She was however no sooner informed that I was there, than she desired I would come up. I did so, and found her sitting in an easy chair near her bed-side; and, in my eyes, as well as all present, seemed in as perfect health as ever she had been. On our inquiring if she felt any inward disorder which should give room for the melancholy apprehensions her message testified, she replied in the negative; 'Yet,' says she, with a little sigh, 'you will very soon, very soon, behold me pass from this world into that eternity, which I doubted but am now assured of.'

A clergyman of her own persuasion, whom she had sent for, that moment coming in we all quitted the room, to leave him at liberty to exercise his function.

It exceeded not half an hour before we were called in again, and she appeared, after having disburdened her conscience, to be more cheerful than before; her eyes, which were as piercing as possible, sparkled with uncommon vivacity; and she told us, she would die with the more satisfaction, as she enjoyed in her last moments the presence of two persons the most agreeable to her in this world, and in the next would be sure of enjoying the society of one, who, in life, had been dearest to her.

We were both beginning to dissuade her from giving way to thoughts which there seemed not the least probability of being verified, when she put a stop to what we were about to urge, by saying, 'Talk no more of that; my time is short, and I would not have the small space allowed me to be with you wasted in vain delusion; know, (continued she,) that I have seen my dear Duchess of Mazarine. I perceived not how she entered, but, turning my eyes towards yonder corner of the room, I saw her stand in the same form and habit she was accustomed to appear in when living: fain would I have spoken, but had not the power of utterance; she took a little circuit round the chamber, seeming rather to swim than walk, then stopped by the side of that Indian chest, and, looking on me with her usual sweetness, 'Beauclair,' said she, 'between the hours of twelve and one this night you will be with me.' The surprise I was in at first being a little abated, I began to ask some questions concerning that future world I was so soon to visit; but, on the opening of my lips for that purpose, she vanished from my sight I know not how.'

The clock was now very near striking twelve; and, as she discovered not the least symptoms of any ailment, we again aimed to remove all apprehensions of a dissolution; but we had scarcely began to speak, when on a sudden her countenance changed, and she cried out, 'Oh! I am sick at heart!' Mrs Ward, who all this while had stood leaning on her chair, applied some drops, but to no effect; she grew still worse; and in about half an hour expired, it being exactly the time the apparition had foretold.

The Marine Spectre

When Mr Walker was setting out on his second trip in the Boscawen private ship of war, in 1745, a report made by the French officers, when the ship was taken, that a gunner's wife had been murdered on board, began now to be looked upon by the men as ominous of the misfortunes which would attend the cruise. One of the seamen, remarkable for his sobriety and good character, one night alarmed the ship, by declaring that he had seen a strange appearance of a woman, who informed him, among other particulars, that the ship would be lost. The story spread among the crew, and laid such hold of the imagination, as would have been attended with the most serious consequences, had not Mr Walker contrived a device for turning it all to ridicule, and with great presence of mind related the following anecdote to the assembled ship's crew.

In June, 1734, Mr Walker lying at anchor at Cadiz, in his ship, the *Elizabeth*, a gentleman of Ireland, whose name was Burnet, was then on board, going to take his passage over to Ireland. The gentleman was a particular acquaintance of Mr Walker, and he was extremely fond of him, being a man of good sense, and very lively in conversation. The night before the affair we speak of happened, the subject turned upon apparitions of deceased friends, in which this person seemed much to believe, and told many strange stories as authorities for them, besides giving some metaphysical arguments, chiefly that the natural fear we had of them proved the soul's confession of them. But Mr Walker, who was entirely of another way of thinking, treated all his arguments with ridicule. Mr Burnet, who was bred a physician, was curious to try how far fancy might be wrought on in an unbeliever, and resolved to prove the power of this natural fear over the senses: a strange way, you will say, to convince the mind by attacking the imagination; or, if it was curiosity to see the operations of fear work on fancy, it was too nice an experiment to anatomize a friend's mind for information only. Or perhaps the humour of the thought was the greatest motive; for he was a man of a gay temper, and frolicsome.

About noon, as they were standing, with more of the ship's company, upon the deck, near the forecastle, looking at some of the governor's guard boats masking fast to a buoy of a ship in bay, in order to watch the money, that it might not be carried out of the country, Mr Burnet proposed, as a plan for a wager, he being a remarkable swimmer, to leap off the gunnel of the ship, and dive all the way quite under water, from the ship to the boats at a distance, and so rise up upon them, to startle the people at watch in them. A wager being laid, he undressed, jumped off, and dived entirely out of sight. Every body crowded forwards, keeping their eyes at the distance where he was expected to come up; but he never rising to their expectation, and the time running past their hopes of ever seeing him more, it was justly concluded he was drowned, and everybody was in the greatest pain and concern; especially those, who by laying the wager, thought themselves in some measure accessory to his death. But he, by skilful diving, having turned the other way behind the ship, and being also very active, got up by the quarter ladder in at the cabin window, whilst everybody was busy and in confusion, at the forward part of the ship; then concealing himself the remaining part of the day in a closet in a state room, wrapped himself up in a linen night-gown of Mr Walker's. Evening coming on, the whole ship's company being very melancholy at the accident, Mr Walker retired with a friend or two to his cabin, where, in their conversation, they often lamented the sad accident and loss of their friend and dear companion, speaking of every merit that he had when living, which is the unenvied praise generally given by our friends, when they can receive nothing else from us.

The supposed dead man remained quite still, and heard more good things said to his memory, than perhaps he would else have ever in his life time heard spoken to his face. As soon as it was night, Mr Walker's company left him; and he being low in spirits went to bed, where lying still pensive on the late loss of his companion and friend, and the moon shining direct through the windows, he perceived the folding doors of the closet to open; and, looking steadfast towards them, saw something which could not fail startling him as he imagined it a representation of a human figure: but recalling his better senses, he was fain to persuade himself, it was only the workings of his disturbed fancy, and away turned his eyes. However they soon again returned in search of the object; and seeing it now plainly advance upon him, in a slow and constant step, he recognised the image of his departed friend. He has not been ashamed to own he felt terrors which shook him to his inmost soul. The mate, who lay in the steerage at the back of the cabin, divided only by a bulk-head, was not yet a-bed; and hearing Mr Walker challenge with a loud and alarmed voice, 'What are you?', ran to him with a candle, and meeting Mr Burnet, in a linen gown, down drops the mate, without so much as an ejaculation. Mr Burnet, now beginning himself to be afraid, runs for a bottle of smelling spirits he knew lay in the window, and applied them to the nose and temples of the swooning mate. Mr Walker, seeing the ghost so very alert and good-natured, began to recover his own apprehension, when Mr Burnet cried out to him, 'Sir, I must ask your pardon; I fear I have carried the jest too far. I swam around and came in the cabin window; I meant, sir, to prove to you the natural awe the bravest must be under at such appearances, and I have, I hope, convinced you in yourself.' 'Sir', says Mr Walker, glad of being awakened from a terrible dream, and belief of his friend's death, 'you have given me a living instance; there needs no proof; but pray take care you do not bring death amongst us in real earnest.' He then lent his aid in the recovery of the poor mate, who, as he retrieved his senses, still relapsed at the sight of Mr Burnet; so that Mr Walker was obliged to make him entirely disappear, and go call others for assistance; which look up some considerable time in doing, every body, as Mr Burnet advanced to them, being more or less surprised: but they were all called to by him, and told the manner of the cheat, and then they were by degrees convinced of his reality; though every one was before thoroughly satisfied of his death.

I being persuaded that this story carries a lesson in it, which speaks for itself, shall conclude it by mentioning this circumstance, that the poor mate never rightly recovered the use of his senses from that hour. Nature had received too great a shock, by which reason was flung from her seat, and could never regain it afterwards; a constant stupidity hung around him, and he could never be brought to look direct at Mr Burnet afterwards, though he was as brave a man as ever went, in all his senses, to face death by day-light.'

Ancient Necromancy

In an Arabic MS in the Royal Library at Paris, containing a description of Egypt, by Macrizy, a singular story is told in these terms.

'The remains of ancient magic are still to be found in the said country. The following circumstance was related on this subject by the Emir Taektabag, who had been governor of Kous under the reign of Mahommed Ben Kalaoun.

'Having arrested a sorceress, I ordered her to show me a specimen of her art. She replied, 'My greatest secret consists in charming the scorpion, by pronouncing the name of a person, whom he is sure to sting and put to death.'

'Well,' said I to her, 'I desire you to make the experiment on me.' Accordingly she took a scorpion; and after having done what she deemed necessary, she let loose the animal, which began to pursue me eagerly, notwithstanding all my endeavours to avoid it. Having placed myself in a seat, in the midst of a reservoir filled with water, the scorpion came to the edge, and endeavoured to reach me. Finding he could not succeed, he crawled up the wall of saloon, and advanced along the ceiling, until having arrived at the spot immediately over me, he dropped and began to run towards me. As I never lost sight of him, as soon as I perceived him at a short distance, I gave him a blow which stretched him dead. After which I ordered the sorceress to be put to death.'

Bonaparte And His Familiar

The 1st of January, 1814, early in the morning, Napoleon shut himself up in his cabinet, bidding Count Mole, then Counsellor of State, and since made Grand Judge of the empire, remain in the next room, and to hinder any person whatever from troubling him, while he was occupied in his cabinet. He looked more thoughtful than usual. He had not long retired to his study, when a tall man, dressed all in red, applied to Mole, pretending that he wanted to speak to the emperor. He was answered, that it was not possible. 'I must speak to him; go and tell him that it is the red man that wants him, and he will admit me.' Awed by the imperious and commanding tone of the strange personage, Mole obeyed reluctantly, and trembling, executed his errand. 'Let him in,' said Bonaparte sternly. Prompted by curiosity, Mole listened at the door, and heard the following curious conversation pass between them.

The red man said, 'This is the third time of my appearing before you: the first time we met was in Egypt, at the battle of the Pyramids. The second, after the battle of Wagram. I then granted you four years more, to terminate the conquest of Europe, or to make a general peace; threatening, that if you did not perform one of these two things, I would withdraw my protection from you. Now I am come for the third and last time, to warn you, that you have but three months to complete the execution of the designs, or to comply with the proposals of the Allies; if you do not achieve the one, or accede to the other, all will be over with you – so remember it well.'

Napoleon then expostulated with him to obtain more time, on the plea that it was impossible, in so short a space, to reconquer what he had lost, or to make peace on honourable terms.

'Do as you please, but my resolution is not to be shaken by entreaties, or otherwise, and I go.'

He opened the door, the emperor followed, entreating him, but to no purpose; the red man would not stop any longer. He went away, casting on his imperial majesty a contemptuous look, and repeating, in a stern voice, 'Three months – no longer.' Napoleon made no reply: but his fiery eyes darted fury, and he returned sullenly to his cabinet, which he did not leave the whole day.

Such were the reports that spread in Paris, three months before the fall of Napoleon Bonaparte, where they caused an unusual sensation, and created a superstitious belief among the people, that he had dealings with infernal spirits, and was bound to fulfil their will or perish. What is more remarkable, in three months the wonderful events justified the red man's words completely; more fortunate than Caesar, or Henry IV of France, these presages did but foretell his ruin, and not his death. Who the man really was who visited Napoleon, in a red dress, has never been known; but that such a person obtained an interview with him, seems to be placed beyond a doubt. Even the French papers, when Bonaparte was deposed, referred to this fact, and remarked, that his mysterious visitant's prophetic threat had been accomplished.

The Radiant Boy: An Apparition Seen By The Late Marquis of Londonderry

It is now more than twenty years since the late Lord Londonderry was, for the first time, on a visit to a gentleman in the north of Ireland. The mansion was such a one as spectres are fabled to inhabit. The apartment, also, which was appropriated to Lord Londonderry, was calculated to foster such a tone of feeling, from its antique appointments; from the dark and richly carved panels of its wainscot; from its yawning width and height of chimney, looking like the open entrance to a tomb, of which the surrounding ornaments appeared to form the sculpture and entablature; from the portraits of grim men and severe-eyed women, arrayed in orderly procession along the walls, and scowling a contemptuous enmity against the degenerate invader of their gloomy bowers and venerable halls; and from the vast dusky, ponderous, and complicated draperies that concealed the windows, and hung with a gloomy grandeur of funeral trappings about the hearse-like piece of furniture that was destined for his bed.

Lord Londonderry examined his chamber; he made himself acquainted with the forms and faces of the ancient possessors of the mansion, as they sat upright in their ebony frame to receive his salutation; and then, after dismissing his valet, he retired to bed. His candles had not long been extinguished when he perceived a light gleaming on the draperies of the lofty canopy over his head. Conscious that there was no fire in the grate – that the curtains were closed – that the chamber had been in perfect darkness but a few minutes before, he supposed that some intruder must have accidentally entered his apartment; and turning hastily round to the side from which the light proceeded, saw, to his infinite astonishment, not the form of any human visitor, but the figure of a fair boy, who seemed to be garmented in rays of mild and tempered glory, which beamed palely from his slender form, like the faint light of the declining moon, and rendered the objects which were nearest to him dimly and indistinctly visible. The spirit stood at some short distance from the side of the bed. Certain that his own faculties were not deceiving him, but suspecting he might be imposed on by the ingenuity of some of the numerous guests who were then visiting in the same house, Lord Londonderry proceeded towards the figure:– it retreated before him;– as he slowly advanced, the form with equal paces slowly retired;– it entered the gloomy arch of the capacious chimney, and then sunk into the earth. Lord Londonderry returned to his bed, but not to rest; his mind was harassed by the consideration of the extraordinary event which had occurred to him.– Was it real?– Was it the work of the imagination?– Was it the result of imposture?– It was all incomprehensible.

He resolved in the morning not to mention the appearance till he should have well observed the manners and countenances of the family: he was conscious that, if any deception had been practiced, its authors would be too delighted with their success to conceal the vanity of their triumph. When the guests assembled at the breakfast table, the eye of Lord Londonderry searched in vain for those latent smiles – those conscious looks – that silent communication between the parties, by which the authors and abettors of such domestic conspiracies are generally betrayed. Every thing apparently proceeded in its ordinary course: the conversation flowed rapidly along from the subjects afforded at some moment, without any of the constraint which marks a party intent upon some secret and more interesting argument, and endeavouring to afford any opportunity for its introduction. At last the hero of the tale found himself compelled to mention the occurrence of the night:– It was most extraordinary:– he feared that he should not be credited:– and then, after all due preparation, the story was related.

Those amongst his auditors who, like himself, were strangers and visitors in the house, were certain that some delusion must have been practiced: the family alone seemed perfectly composed and calm. At last, the gentleman whom Lord Londonderry was visiting interrupted their various surmises on the subject, by saying – 'The circumstance which you have just recounted must naturally appear very extraordinary to those who have not long been inmates of my dwelling, and not conversant with the legends of my family; and to those who are, the event which happened will only serve as the corroboration of an old tradition that has long been related of the apartment in which you slept. You have seen the Radiant Boy – be content – it is an omen of prosperous fortunes. I would rather the subject should no more be mentioned.' And here the affair ended.

Extraordinary Instance Of Second Sight

A gentleman connected with the family of Dr Ferriar, an officer in the army and certainly addicted to no superstition, was quartered early in life, in the middle of the last century, near the castle of a gentleman in the north of Scotland, who was supposed to possess the second sight. Strange rumours were afloat respecting the old chieftain: he had spoken to an apparition, which ran along the battlements of the house, and had never been cheerful afterwards: his prophetic vision excited surprise even in that region of credulity, and retired habits favoured the popular opinion. One day, while the officer was reading a play to the ladies of the family, the chief, who had been walking across the room, stopped suddenly, and assumed the look of a seer: he rang the bell, and ordered the groom to saddle a horse, to proceed immediately to a seat in the neighbourhood, and to inquire after the health of Lady ———; if the account were favourable, he then directed him to call at another castle, to ask after another lady whom he named.

The reader immediately closed his book, and declared he would not proceed until these abrupt orders were explained, as he was confident they were produced by the second sight. The chief was very, very unwilling to explain himself, but at length he owned that the door had appeared to open, and that a little old woman, without a head, had entered the room; that the apparition indicated that the sudden death of some person of his acquaintance, and the only two persons who resembled the figure were those ladies after whose health he had sent to inquire.

A few hours afterwards the servant returned, with an account that one of the ladies had died, of an apoplectic fit, about the time when the vision appeared.

At another time the chief was confined to his bed by indisposition, and my friend was reading to him in a stormy winter night, while the fishing boat belonging to the castle was at sea. The old gentlemen repeatedly expressed much anxiety respecting his people, and at last exclaimed:– 'My boat is lost!' The colonel replied:– 'How do you know it, sir?' He was answered:– 'I see two of the boatmen bringing in the third drowned, all dripping wet, and laying him down close besides your chair.' The chair was shifted with great precipitation: in the course of the night the fishermen returned, with the corpse of one of the boatmen.

No Spectre

Monsieur de Conange, on a wandering excursion which he was making with a friend through one of the French provinces, found it necessary one night to take refuge from a storm, in an inn which had little else to recommend it, but that the host was well known to M. de Conange. This man had all the inclination in the world to accommodate the travellers to their satisfaction, but unfortunately he possessed not the power. The situation was desolate, and the few chambers the house contained were already occupied by other travellers. There remained unengaged only a single parlour on the ground floor, with a closet adjoining, with which, inconvenient as they were, M. de Conange and his friend were obliged to content themselves. The closet was provided with a very uninviting bed for the latter, while they supped together in the parlour, where it was decided that M. de Conange was to sleep. As they purposed departing very early in the morning, they soon retired to their separate beds, and ere long fell into a profound sleep.

Short, however, had been M. de Conange's repose, when he was disturbed by the voice of his fellow traveller, crying out that something was strangling him. Though he heard his friend speak to him, he could not for some time sufficiently rouse himself from his drowsiness, to awaken a full sense of the words that his friend had uttered. This was a voice of distress, he now perfectly understood, and he called anxiously to inquire what was the matter; no answer was returned, no sound was heard at all, all was still as death.

Now seriously alarmed M. de Conange threw himself out of bed, and taking up his candle, proceeded to the closet. What was the horror and astonishment, when he beheld his friend lying senseless beneath the strangling grasp of a dead man, loaded with chains! The cries of distress, which this dreadful sight called forth, soon brought the host to his assistance, whose fear and astonishment acquitted him of being in any way an actor in the tragic scene before them. It was, however, a more pressing duty to endeavour to recover the senseless traveller, than to unravel the mysterious event which had reduced him to that state. The barber of the village was therefore immediately sent for, and in the meantime, they extricated the traveller from the grasp of the man, whose hand had in death fastened on his throat with a force which rendered it difficult to unclench. While performing this, they happily ascertained that the vital spark still faintly glowed in the heart of the traveller, although wholly fled from that of his assaulter. The operation of bleeding, which the barber now arrived to perform, gave that spark new vigour, and he was shortly after put to bed out of danger, and left to all that could be of service to him – repose.

M. de Conange then felt himself at liberty to satisfy his curiosity, in developing the mystery of this strange adventure, which was quickly effected by his host. This man informed him that the deceased was his groom, who had within a few days exhibited strong proofs of his mental derangement, as it render it absolutely necessary to use coercive measures, to prevent his either doing mischief to himself or others, and that he had in consequence been confined or chained in the stables; but that it was evident his fetters had proved too weak to resist the strength of frenzy, and that in liberating himself, he had passed through a little door, imprudently left unlocked, which led from the saddle room into the closet in which the traveller slept, and had entered it to die with such frightful effects on his bed.

When in the course of a few days, M. de Conange's friend was able to converse, he acknowledged that never in his life had he suffered so much, and that he was confident had be not fainted, madness must have been the consequence of a prolonged state of terror.

Apparition of Marshal Saxe

A man of the name of Schrepfer, who originally resided at Leipsic, of which city he was a native, and where he kept a coffee-house, pretended to study magic, and to have acquired many secrets connected with that imaginary science. He boldly asserted that he had intercourse with, and a control over spirits, whom he could summon, command, and cause to disappear, if not altogether at his pleasure, yet by force of his inventions. Pretensions so extraordinary, sustained by some exhibitions which impressed the spectators with astonishment, soon procured him no little reputation.

Schrepfer, about this time, while he still resided at Leipsic, had offered Prince Charles of Saxony, who ordered an officer belonging to his household to repair to Leipsic, and there to give to Schrepfer, in his name, personal chastisement. But, while this gentleman inflicted it, Schrepfer threw himself on his knees, and loudly invoked his invisible allies to come to his assistance: and the officer was so much alarmed at the invocation, and its possible consequences, as to quit the chamber with precipitation. A circumstance so degrading to Schrepfer, induced him to leave Leipsic.

After an absence of some time, he appeared in Dresden, where his pretences to skill in magic attracting many followers, his reputation speedily reached Prince Charles, and induced that prince to make every exertion in obliterating the recollection of the indignity lately offered him. He did not hesitate to go in person to the inn where Schrepfer lodged; solicited his pardon and offered every amends.

Schrepfer having accepted the apologies, the prince then requested to see some proofs of his supernatural art. It is said he exhibited many; but the most difficult operation of magic in all ages, has been to raise departed spirits from the tomb; a prodigy which Schrepfer made no secret of his ability to perform. Prince Charles having earnestly besought it, obtained at length a reluctant promise to present before his eyes an apparition. It only remained, therefore, to fix the spirit to be summoned. After long consideration, the Chevalier de Saxe was named, and Schrepfer undertook to produce his ghost before a select company. The place chosen for the experiment was Prince Charles's palace in Dresden; and the strictest secrecy was observed previous to the affair.

The Chevalier de Saxe died only a few years ago, at his palace, which his nephew Prince Charles, who was his principle heir, occupied after his decease. As he left no issue, he was supposed to have amassed great sums. Reports had been circulated, that money was concealed in the palace; and if his spirit could be compelled to appear, that interesting secret might be extorted from him. This motive prompted Prince Charles to name his uncle, as the object of the experiment.

On the appointed night, the company assembled. They were nineteen in number, persons of consideration, character and respectability. The first object of all present was to secure the windows and doors. They did so; and were satisfied that nothing except violence could procure access or entrance.

Schrepfer then acquainted them, that the act which he was about to perform would demand all their firmness;

and advised them to fortify their nerves by partaking of a bowl of punch, which was placed upon the table. Several of them very readily followed it; but one gentleman declined the advice. 'I am come here,' said he to Schrepfer, 'to be present at raising an apparition. Either I will see all or nothing. My resolution is taken, and no inducement can make me put any thing within my lips.' Another of the company placed himself close to the principal door, in order to watch if any one attempted to open or force it. These preparatory steps being taken, the great work began with the utmost solemnity.

Schrepfer commenced it, by retiring into a corner of the gallery, where kneeling down, with many mysterious ceremonies, he invoked the spirits to come to his aid. A very considerable time elapsed before they obeyed; during which interval, he laboured apparently under great agitation of body and mind being covered with a violent sweat, and almost in convulsions. At length, a loud clatter was heard at all the windows on the outside; which was soon followed by another noise, resembling more the effect produced by a number of wet fingers drawn over the edge of glasses, than any thing else to which it could well be compared. The sound announced, as he said, the arrival of his good or protecting spirits, and seemed to encourage him to proceed. A short time afterwards, a yelling was heard of a frightful and unusual nature, which came, he declared, from the malignant spirits, whose presence was necessary and indispensable to the completion of the catastrophe.

The company were now petrified with horror; and Schrepfer continuing his invocations, the door suddenly opened with violence, and something that resembled a black ball or globe, rolled into the middle of the room.

It was invested with smoke or cloud, in the midst of which appeared to be a human face, like the countenance of the Chevalier de Saxe. From this form issued a loud and angry voice, which exclaimed in German, 'Carl, was wolte du mit me? Why dost thou disturb me?' Language, as may be supposed, can ill describe the consternation produced among the spectators at such a sight. The prince, whose impious curiosity had summoned his uncle's ghost, and to whom the spectre principally addressed itself, far from manifesting coolness, or attempting reply, betrayed the strongest marks of horror and contrition. Throwing himself on his knees, he called on God for mercy; whilst others of the terrified party earnestly besought the magician to give the only remaining proof of his art for which they were now anxious, by dismissing the apparition. But near an hour elapsed, before, by the force of his invocations, the spectre could be compelled to disappear. Nay, when at length Schrepfer had succeeded in dismissing it; the moment that the company began to assume a degree of serenity, the door which had been closed, burst open again, and the same hideous form presented itself anew to their eyes. The most resolute and collected among them, were not proof to its second appearance, and a scene of universal terror ensued. Schrepfer, however, by reiterated exorcisms or exertions, finally dismissed the apparition. The terrified spectators soon dispersed, overcome with amazement and fully satisfied with Schrepfer's supernatural powers.

Schrepfer did not long enjoy his celebrity, and his death is not the least extraordinary part of the history. These gentlemen whom he had in some measure initiated into its mysteries (for he professed to instruct in the science of magic) were promised by him an exhibition more wonderful than any at which they had yet assisted. For this purpose they attended him into the wood of Rosendaal, which is a small distance from the gates of Leipsic. It was summer, before the sun rose, between three and four in the morning. When they came to a certain part of the grove, he desired them to stay a little, while he went on one side to make the requisite invocations. After waiting a few minutes, they heard the report of a pistol. Running to the spot, they found that he had shot himself, and was already without sense. He soon expired.

Apparition Of Lord Tyrone To Lady Beresford

Lord Tyrone and Miss ————— were born in Ireland, and were left orphans in their infancy to the care of the same person, by whom they were both educated in the principles of deism.

Their guardian dying when they were each about fourteen years of age, they fell into very different hands. The persons on whom the care of them now devolved used every means to eradicate the erroneous principles they had imbibed, and to persuade them to embrace revealed religion, but in vain. Their arguments were insufficient to convince, though they were strong enough to stagger their former faith. Though separated from each other, their friendship was unalterable, and they continued to regard each other with a sincere and fraternal affection. After some years were elapsed, and both were grown up, they made a solemn promise to each other that whichever should die first, would, if permitted, appear to the other, to declare what religion was most approved of by the Supreme Being.

Miss ———— was shortly after addressed by Sir Martin Beresford, to whom she was, after a few years, married, but a change of condition had no power to alter their friendship. The families visited each other, and often for some weeks together. A short time after one of these visits, Sir Martin remarked, that when his lady came down to breakfast, her countenance was disturbed, and inquired of her health. She assured him she was quite well. He then asked her if she had hurt her wrist: 'Have you sprained it?' said he, observing a black ribbon round it. She answered in the negative, and added, 'Let me conjure you, Sir Martin, never to inquire the cause of my wearing this ribbon; you will never see me without it. If it concerned you as a husband to know, I would not for a moment conceal it: I never in my life denied you a request, but of this I entreat you to forgive me the refusal, and never to urge me further on the subject.' 'Very well,' said he, smiling, 'since you beg me so earnestly, I will inquire no more.'

The conversation here ended; but breakfast was scarce over when Lady Beresford eagerly if the post was come; she was told it had not. In a few minutes she ran and repeated the enquiry. She was again answered as at first. 'Do you expect letters?' said Sir Martin, 'that you are so anxious for the arrival of the post?' 'I do,' she answered, 'I expect to hear that Lord Tyrone is dead; he died last Tuesday at four o'clock.' 'I never in my life,' said Sir Martin, 'believed you superstitious; some idle dream has surely thus alarmed you.' At that instant the servant entered and delivered to them a letter sealed with black. 'It is as I expected,' exclaimed Lady Beresford, 'Lord Tyrone is dead.' Sir Martin opened the letter; it came from Lord Tyrone's steward, and contained the melancholy intelligence of his master's death, and on the very day and hour Lady Beresford had before specified.

Sir Martin begged Lady Beresford to compose herself, and she assured him she felt much easier than she had done for a long time; and added, 'I can communicate intelligence to you which I know will prove welcome; I can assure you, beyond the possibility of a doubt, that I shall in some months present you with a son.' Sir Martin received this news with greatest joy. After some months, Lady Beresford was delivered of a son; she had before been the mother of only two daughters. Sir Martin survived the birth of his son little more than four years. After his decease his widow seldom left home; she visited no family but that of a clergyman who resided in the same village; with them she frequently passed a few hours every day; the rest of her time was spent in solitude, and she appeared determined to banish all other society. The clergyman's family consisted of himself, his wife, and one son, who, at the time of Sir Martin's death, was quite a youth; to this son, however, she was after a few years married, notwithstanding the disparity of youth and the manifest imprudence of a connection so unequal in every point of view. Lady Beresford was treated by her young husband with contempt and cruelty, while at the same time his conduct evinced him the most abandoned libertine, utterly destitute of every principle of virtue and humanity. By this, her second husband, she had two daughters; after which, such was the baseness of his conduct, that she insisted on a separation. They parted for a few years, when so great was the contrition he expressed for his former conduct, that, won over by his supplications, promises, and entreaties, she was induced to pardon, and once more to reside with him, and was in time the mother of a son.

The day on which she had laid-in a month, being the anniversary of her birth-day, she sent for Lady Betty Cobb (of whose friendship she had long been possessed), and a few other friends to request them to spend the day with her. About seven, the clergyman by whom she had been christened, and with whom she had all her life been inti-mate, came into the room to inquire after her health. She told him she was perfectly well, and requested him to spend the day with them; 'For,' said she, 'this is my birth day. I am forty-eight to-day.' 'No, madam,' answered the clergyman, 'you are mistaken; your mother and myself have had many disputes concerning your age, and I have at last discovered that I was right. I happened to go last week into the parish were you were born; I was resolved to put an end to this dispute; I searched the register, and find that you are but forty-seven this day.' 'You have signed my death warrant!' she exclaimed.

'I have but a few hours to live. I must, therefore, entreat you to leave me immediately, as I have something impor-tant to settle before I die.' When the clergyman had left her, Lady Beresford sent to forbid the company coming, and at the same time to request Lady Betty Cobb, and her son (of whom Sir Martin was the father, and was then about twenty-two years of age), to come to her apartment imme-diately. Upon their arrival, having ordered the attendants to quit the room, 'I have something,' said she, 'of the great-est importance to communicate to you both before I die, a period which is not far distant. You, Lady Betty, are no stranger to the friendship which subsisted between Lord Tyrone and myself: we were educated under the same roof, and in the same principles of deism. When the friends, into whose hands we afterwards fell, endeavoured to persuade us to embrace revealed religion, their arguments, though insufficient to convince, were powerful enough to stagger our former feelings, and to leave us wavering between the two opinions: in this perplexing state of doubt and uncertainty, we made a solemn promise to each other, that which died first should (if permitted) appear to the other, and declare which religion was most acceptable to God: accordingly, one night, while Sir Martin and myself were in bed, I suddenly woke and discovered Lord Tyrone sitting by my bedside. I screamed out and endeavoured to awake Sir Martin, "For heaven's sake," I exclaimed, "Lord Tyrone, by what means, or for what reason, came you hither at this time of night?" "Have you then forgotten our promise?" said he. "I died last Tuesday at four o'clock, and been permitted by the Supreme Being to appear to you, to assure you the revealed religion is true, and the only religion by which we can be saved. I am further suffered to inform you that you will soon produce a son; who, it is decreed, will marry my daughter: not many years after his birth Sir Martin will die, and you will marry again, and to a man by whose ill treatment you will be rendered miserable: you will have two daughters, and afterwards a son, in child-birth of whom you will die in the forty-seventh year of your age."

"'Just heavens!" I exclaimed, "and cannot I prevent this?" "Undoubtedly you may," returned the spectre, "you are a free agent, and may prevent it all by resisting every temptation to a second marriage; but your passions are strong, you know not their power; hitherto you have had no trials. More I am not permitted to reveal, but if after this warning you persist in your infidelity, your lot in another world will be miserable indeed!" "May I not ask," said I, "if you are happy?" "Had I been otherwise," he replied, "I should not be permitted to appear to you." "I may then infer that you are happy?" He smiled. "But how," said I, "when morning comes, shall I know that your appearance to me has been real, and not the mere representation of my own imagination?" "Will not the news of my death be sufficient to convince you?" "No," I returned, "I might have had such a dream, and that dream accidentally came to pass. I will have some stronger proofs of its reality." "You shall," said he, and waving his hand, the bed-curtains, which were of crimson velvet, were instantly drawn through a large iron hoop by which the tester of the bed was suspended. "In that," said he, "you cannot be mistaken; no mortal arm could have performed this." "True," said I, "but sleeping we are often of far more strength than when awake; though waking I could not have done it, asleep I might; and I shall still doubt." "Here is a pocket-book," said he; "in it I will write my name: you know my hand writing." I replied, "Yes." He wrote with a pencil on one side of the leaves. "Still," said I, "in the morning I may doubt; though waking I could not imitate the hand, asleep I might." "You are hard of belief," said he: "it would injure you irreparably; it is not for spirits to touch mortal flesh." "I do not," said I, "regard a light blemish." "You are a woman of courage," replied he, "hold out your hand." I did: he touched my wrist: his hand was cold as marble: in a moment the sinews shrunk up, every nerve withered. "Now," said he, "while you live, let no mortal eye behold that wrist: to see it is sacrilege." He stopped; I turned to him again; he was gone.

'During the time I had conversed my thoughts were perfectly calm and collected, but the moment he was gone, I felt chilled with horror, the very bed moved under me. I endeavoured, in vain, to wake Sir Martin, all my attempts were ineffectual, and in this state of agitation and terror I lay for some time, when a shower of tears came to my relief, and I dropped asleep. In the morning, Sir Martin arose and dressed himself as usual, without perceiving the state the curtains remained in. When I awoke I found Sir Martin gone down; I arose, and having put on my clothes, went to the gallery adjoining the apartment, and took from thence a long broom (such as cornices are swept with), by the help of this I took down with some difficulty the curtains, as I imagined the extraordinary position might excite suspicions in the family. I then went to the bureau, took up my pocket-book, and bound a piece of black ribbon round my wrist. When I came down, the agitations of my mind had left an impression on my countenance too visible to pass unobserved by my husband. He instantly remarked it and asked the case; I informed him Lord Tyrone was no more, that he died at the hour of four on the preceding Tuesday, and desired him never to question me more respecting the black ribbon; which he kindly desisted from after.

'You, my son, as had been foretold, I afterwards brought into the world, and in a little time after your birth your lamented father expired in my arms. After this melancholy event, I determined as the only probable chance to avoid the sequel of the prediction, for ever to abandon all society; to give up every pleasure resulting from it, and pass the remainder of my days in solitude and retirement. But few can long endure to exist in a state of perfect sequestration: I began an intimacy with a family, and one alone; nor could I then foresee the fatal consequences which afterwards resulted from it. Little did I think that their son, their only son, then a mere youth, would form the person destined by fate to prove my destruction.

'In a very few years I ceased to regard him with indifference; I endeavoured by every possible way to conquer a passion the fatal effects of which I knew too well. I had fondly imagined I had overcome its influence, when the evening of one fatal day terminated my fortitude, and plunged me in a moment down that abyss I had so long been meditating to shun. He had often solicited his parents for leave to go into the army, and at last obtained permission, and came to bid adieu before his departure. The instant he entered the room he fell upon his knees at my feet, told me he was miserable, and that I alone was the cause. At that moment my fortitude forsook me, I gave myself up for lost, and regarding my fate as inevitable, without further hesitation consented to a union, the immediate result of which I knew to be misery, and its end death. The conduct of my husband, after a few years, amply justified a separation, and I hoped by this means to avoid the fatal sequel of the prophecy; but won over by his reiterated entreaties, I was prevailed upon to pardon, and once more reside with him, though not till after I had, as I thought, passed my forty-seventh year.

'But alas! I have this day heard from an indisputable authority, that I have hitherto lain under a mistake with regard to my age, and that I am but forty-seven today. Of the near approach of my death then I entertain not the slightest doubt; but I do not dread its arrival. When I am dead, as the necessity of concealment closes with my life, I would wish that you, Lady Betty, would unbind my wrist, take from thence the black ribbon; and let my son with yourself behold it.'

Lady B. then expressed a wish to lay down on the bed and endeavour to compose herself to sleep. Lady Betty Cobb and her son immediately called her domestics, and quitted the room, having first desired them to watch their mistress attentively, and if they observed the smallest change in her, to call instantly. An hour passed, and all was quiet in the room. They listened at the door and every thing remained still, but in half an hour more a bell rang violently; they flew to her apartment, but before they reached the door, they heard the servants exclaim, 'Oh, she is dead!' Lady Betty then bade her servants for a few minutes to quit the room, and herself with Lady Beresford's son approached the bed of his mother; they knelt down by the side of it; Lady Betty then lifted up her hand and untied the ribbon; the wrist was found exactly as Lady Beresford had described it, every sinew shrunk, every nerve withered.

Lady Beresford's son, as had been predicted, is since married to Lord Tyrone's daughter. The black ribbon and pocket-book were formerly in the possession of Lady Betty Cobb, Marlborough Buildings, Bath, who, during her long life, was ever ready to attest the truth of this narration, as are, to the present hour, the whole of the Tyrone and Beresford families.

The Scalping Knife and Tomahawk, Or Mode
Of Warfare Among American Indians

As the American tribes are early possessed with a notion that war ought to be the chief business of their lives, that there is nothing more desirable than the reputation of being a great warrior, and that the scalps of their enemies, or a number of prisoners, are alone esteemed valuable, it is not to be wondered at, that the young Indians are continually restless and uneasy if their ardour is repressed, and they are kept in a state of inactivity.

When the chiefs find any occasion for making war, they endeavour to arouse their prejudices, and by that means soon excite their warriors to take arms. For this purpose they make use of their martial eloquence, nearly in the following words, which never fail of proving effectual: 'The bones of our deceased countrymen lie uncovered, they call out to us to revenge their wrongs, and we must satisfy their request. Their spirits cry out against us. They must be appeased. The genii, who are the guardians of our honour, inspire us with a resolution to seek the enemies of our murdered brothers. Let us go and devour those by whom they were slain. Sit here no longer inactive; give way to the impulse of your natural vigour, cause the forest to resound with your songs, console the spirits of the dead, and tell them they shall be revenged.'

Animated by these exhortations, the warriors snatch their arms in a transport of fury, sing the songs of war, and burn with impatience to imbrue their hands in the blood of their enemies.

Sometimes private chiefs assemble small parties and make excursions against those with whom they are at war, or such as have injured them. A single warrior, prompted by revenge or a desire to show his prowess, will march unattended for several hundred miles, to surprise or cut off a straggling party.

The chief warrior of a nation does not on all occasions head the party himself, he frequently deputes a warrior of whose valour and prudence he has a good opinion. The person thus fixed on being first bedaubed with black, observes a fast of several days, during which he invokes the Great Spirit, or deprecates the anger of the evil ones, holding, while it lasts, no converse with any of his tribe.

He is particularly careful at the same time to observe his dreams, for on these do they suppose their success will in a great measure depend; and from the firm persuasion every Indian, actuated by his own presumptuous thoughts, is impressed with, that he shall march forth to certain victory, these are generally favourable to his wishes.

After he has fasted as long as custom prescribes, he assembles the warriors, and holding a belt of wampum in his hand, he thus addresses them:

'Brothers! by the inspiration of the Great Spirit I now speak to you, and by him I am prompted to carry into execution the intentions which I am about to disclose to you. The blood of our deceased brothers is not yet wiped away; their bodies are not yet covered, and I am going to perform this duty to them.'

Having then made known all the motives that induced him to take up arms against the nation with whom they are about to engage, he thus proceeds: 'I have therefore resolved to march through the war-paths to surprise them. We will eat their flesh, and drink their blood; we will take scalps, and make prisoners; and should we perish in this glorious enterprise we shall not for ever be hidden in the dust, for this belt shall be a recompense for him who buries the dead.' Having said this he lays the belt on the ground, and he who takes it up declares himself his lieutenant, and is considered as the second in command; this, however, is only done by some distinguished warrior who has a right by the number of scalps, to the post.

The Apparition Of The Murdered Boy

At the commencement of the French Revolution, Lady Pennyman and her two daughters retired to Lisle, where they had hired a large and handsome house at a very trifling rent. During their residence in this abode, the lady received from her husband, Sir John Pennyman, a draft for a considerable sum, which she carried to the banker of the town, and requested to have cashed. The man, as is much the custom on the continent, gave her a large portion of silver in exchange. As Lady Pennyman was proceeding to pay some visits, she requested that the banker would send the money to her house, of which she described the situation. The parcel was instantly committed to the care of a porter; and, on the lady's inquiring of him whether he understood, from her directions, the place to which his charge was to be conveyed, the man replied that he was perfectly aware of the place designated, that it was called the 'Haunted House'. The latter part of this answer was addressed to the banker in a low tone of voice, but was overheard by Lady Pennyman: she paid, however, no attention to the words, and naturally supposed that the report connected with her habitation was one of those which are raised by the ignorant respecting every dwelling which is long untenanted, or remarkable for its antiquity.

A few weeks afterwards, the words were recalled to her recollection in a manner that surprised her: the housekeeper, with many apologies for being obliged to mention any thing that might appear so idle and absurd, came to the apartment in which her mistress was sitting; and said that two of the servants, who accompanied her ladyship from England, had that morning given warning, and expressed a determination of quitting her ladyship's service, on account of the mysterious noises by which they had been, night after night, disturbed and terrified. 'I trust, Carter,' replied Lady Pennyman, 'that you have too much good sense to be alarmed on your own account by any of these superstitions and visionary fears; and pray exert yourself in endeavouring to tranquillize the apprehensions of others, and persuading them to continue in their places.' The persuasion of Carter was ineffectual: the servants insisted that the noises which had alarmed them were not the operation of any earthly beings, and persevered in their resolution of returning to their native country.

The room from which the sounds were supposed to have proceeded was at a distance from Lady Pennyman's apartment, and immediately over those which were occupied by the two female servants, who themselves had been terrified by them, and whose report has spread a general panic through the rest of the family. To quiet the alarm, Lady Pennyman resolved on leaving her own chamber for a time, and establishing herself in the one which had lately been occupied by the domestics.

The room above was a long spacious apartment, which appeared to have been for a length of time deserted. In the centre of the chamber was a large iron cage: it was an extraordinary piece of furniture to find in any mansion, but the legend which the servants had collected respecting it appeared to be still more extraordinary: it was said that a late proprietor of the house, a young man of enormous property, had in his minority been confined in that apartment by his uncle and guardian, and there hastened to a premature death by the privations and cruelties to which he was exposed: those cruelties had been practiced under the pretence of necessary correction. It was alleged that he was idle, stubborn, inattentive, and of an untoward disposition, which nothing but severity could improve. In his boyhood, frequent chastisements, continued application, and the refusal of any interval of relaxation were vain essayed to urge and goad him to the grave, and to place his uncle in possession of the inheritance: his constitution struggled with the tyranny of his unnatural relation, and, wasted as it was by the unmitigated oppression, still resisted with an admirable vitality the efforts which were ingeniously aimed against his existence.

As he drew nearer the age in which he would have been legally delivered from the dangers and impositions of his uncle, his life was subjected to more violent and repeated severities; every, even the slightest offence was succeeded by the most rigorous inflictions. The iron cage was threatened, was ordered, was erected in the upper chamber. At first, for a few weeks, it remained as an object of terror only: it was menaced that the next transgression of his guardian's wishes would be punished by a day's imprisonment in that narrow circle, without the possibility of rest, or permission of refreshment. Twice the cage was threatened and remitted, from an affected show of mercy, and the better to cover and to palliate the premeditated enormities: the youth, who was about sixteen, from the dread of this terrible affliction, applied himself with sleepless diligence to labours difficult to be accomplished, and extended, purposefully extended, beyond the capacity of the student: his lessons were exacted, not in proportion to his abilities, but his endeavours and performance.

The taskmaster eventually conquered: then followed the imprisonment, and the day without food. Again the imposition was set; again executed with painful exertion: again lengthened; again discovered to be impracticable, and again visited with the iron cage and the denial of necessary subsistence. The savage purpose of thus murdering the boy, under the pretence of a strict attention to his interest or his improvement, was at last successful: the lad was declared to be incorrigible; there was a feigned necessity of more severe correction: he was sentenced to two days' captivity and privation. So long an abstinence from food and rest was more than his enfeebled frame and his broken spirits could endure; and, on his uncle's arriving, with the show of an hypocritical leniency, an hour previous to the appointed time, to deliver him from the residue of his punishment, it was found that death had anticipated the false mercy, and had for ever emancipated the innocent sufferer from the hands of the oppressor.

The wealth was won; but it was an unprofitable acquisition to him, who had so dearly purchased it:– 'What profit is it,' demands the voice of Revelation, 'if a man should gain the whole world, and lose his own soul?' His conscience haunted him: the form of the dead and inoffensive boy was constantly before him. His dreams represented to his view the playful and beautiful looks that won all eyes before him, while his parents were yet alive to cheer and delight him: and then the vision of his sleep would change: and he would see his calm suffering and his silent tears, and his patient endurance of his indefatigable exertions in attempting the accomplishment of difficult exactions, and his pale cheek, and his wasted limbs, and his spiritless countenance; and then, at last, there was the rigid, ebony, and distorted form, the glazed open eye, the mouth violently compressed, and the clenched hands, on which his view had rested for a moment, when all his wicked hopes had attained their most sanguine consummation, as he surveyed the corpse of his murdered relative. These recollections banished him from his home; the mansion was left tenantless; and 'till Lady Pennyman had ignorantly engaged it, all had dreaded to become inmates of a dwelling which had been fatal to one possessor, and shunned as destructive to the tranquillity of his heir.

On the first night or two of Lady Pennyman's being established in her new apartment, she met with no interruption; nor was her sleep in the least disturbed by any of those mysterious noises in the Cage Chamber (for so it was commonly called in the family) which she has been induced to expect by the representations of the departed servants. This quiet, however, was of very short duration: one night she was awakened from her sleep by the sound of a slow and measured step, that appeared to be pacing the chamber overhead: it continued to move backwards and forwards with nearly the same constant and regular motion for rather more than an hour – perhaps Lady Pennyman's agitation may have deceived her, and induced her to think the time longer than it really was. It at length ceased: morning dawned upon her. The lady naturally felt distressed by the occurrence of the night; it was in every point of view alarming: if she doubted its being the effect of any preternatural communication, there was only another alternative, which was almost equally distressing – to suppose that there were means of entering the house, which were known to strangers, though concealed from the inhabitants. She went down to breakfast, after framing a resolution not to mention the event.

Lady Pennyman and her daughters had nearly completed their breakfast before her son, a young man who had lately returned from sea, descended from his apartment. 'My dear Charles,' said his mother, 'I wonder you are not ashamed of your indolence and your want of gallantry, to suffer your sisters and myself to finish breakfast before you are ready to join us.' – 'Indeed, madam,' he replied, 'it is not my fault if I am late: I have not had any sleep all night. There have been people knocking at my door and peeping into my room every half-hour since I went up-stairs to bed: I presume they wanted to see if my candle was extinguished. If this be the case, it is really very distressing; as I certainly never gave you any occasion to suspect I should be careless in such a light to the domestics.' – 'Indeed, my dear, the interruption has taken place entirely without my knowledge. I assure you it is not by any order of mine that your room has been looked into: I cannot think who could induce any servant of mine to be guilty of such a liberty. Are you certain that you have not mistaken the nature and origin of the sound?' – 'Oh, yes; there could be no mistake: I was perfectly awake when the interruption took place, and afterwards it was so frequently repeated as to prevent the possibility of my sleeping.'

More complaints from the housekeeper; no servants would remain; every individual of the family had his tale of terror to increase the apprehensions of the rest. Lady Pennyman began herself to be alarmed. Mrs Atkins, a very dear and approved friend, came on a visit to her: she communicated the subject which had so recently disturbed the family, and requested her advice. Mrs Atkins, a woman devoid of every kind of superstitious fear, and of tried courage, understanding, and resolution, determined at once to silence all the stories that had been fabricated respecting the Cage Room, and to allay their terrors by adopting that apartment for her own bed-chamber during the remainder of her residence at Lisle. It was in vain to oppose her purpose: she declared that no half measure could be equally effectual: that, if any of the family were to sleep there, though their rest should be perfectly undisturbed, it would have no efficacy in tranquillising the agitation of the family; since the servants would naturally accuse either Lady Pennyman or her son of being interested witnesses, and doubt of the fact of their having reposed in the centre of the ghost's dominions, without undergoing any punishment for the temerity of their invading them. A bed was accordingly placed in the apartment. The Cage Room was rendered as comfortable as possible on so short a notice; and Mrs Atkins retired to rest, attended by her favourite spaniel, saying, as she bade them all good night, 'I and my dog, I flatter myself, are equal to compete with a myriad of ghosts; so let me entreat you to be under no apprehensions for the safety of Rose and myself.'

Mrs Atkins examined her chamber in every imaginable direction: she sounded every panel of the wainscot, to prove that there was no hollowness, which might argue a concealed passage: and, having bolted the door of the Cage Room, retired to rest, confident that she was secure against every material visitor, and totally incredulous of the airy encroachments of all spiritual beings. Her assurance was doomed to be short-lived: she had only been a few minutes asleep, when her dog, which lay by the bedside, leaped howling and terrified, upon the bed; the door of the chamber slowly opened, and a pale, thin, sickly youth came in, cast his eyes mildly towards her, walked up to the iron cage in the middle of the room, and then leaned in the melancholy attitude of one resolving in his mind the sorrow of a cheerless and unblest existence: after a while he again withdrew, and retired by the way he entered.

Mrs Atkins, on witnessing his departure, felt the return of her resolution: she was re-assured in her original belief in the impossibility of all spiritual visitations: she persuaded herself to believe the figure the work of some skilful impostor, and she determined on following its footsteps: she took up her chamber lamp, and hastened to put her design into execution. On reaching the door, to her infinite surprise, she discovered it to be fastened, as she has herself left it, on retiring to bed. On withdrawing the bolt and opening the door, she saw the back of the youth descending the staircase: she followed, 'till, on reaching the foot of the stairs, the form appeared to sink into the earth. It was in vain to attempt concealing the occurrences of the night: her voice, her manner, the impossibility of sleeping a second time in the ill-omened chamber, would necessarily betray that something of a painful and mysterious nature had occurred.

The event was related to Lady Pennyman: she determined to remain no longer in her present habitation. The man of whom the house had been engaged was spoken to on the subject: he became extremely violent – said it was no time for the English to indulge their imaginations – insinuated something of the guillotine – and bade her, at her peril, drop a single expression to the injury of his property. While she remained in France, no word was uttered upon the subject; she framed an excuse for her abrupt departure: another residence was offered in the vicinity of Lisle, which she engaged, on the pretext of its being better calculated to the size of her family; and at once relinquished her habitation, and with it every preternatural occasion for anxiety.

The Accusing Spirit

A farmer, on his return from the market at Southam, in the county of Warwick, was murdered. A man went the next morning to his wife, and enquired if her husband came home the evening before; she replied no, and that she was under the utmost anxiety and terror on that account. Your terror, said he, cannot equal mine; for last night, as I lay in bed, quite awake, the apparition of your husband appeared to me, shewed me several ghastly stabs in his body, told me he had been murdered by such a person, and his carcass thrown into such a marl-pit.

The alarm was given, the pit searched, the body found, and the wounds answered the description of them. The man, whom the ghost had accused, was apprehended and committed on a violent suspicion of murder. His trial came on at Warwick, before the Lord Chief Justice Raymond, when the jury would have convicted, as rashly as the justices of the peace had committed him, had not the judge checked them. He addressed himself to them in words to this effect: 'I think, gentlemen, you seem inclined to lay more stress on the evidence of an apparition that it will bear. I can not say that I give much credit to these kind of stories: but, be that as it will, we have no right to follow our own private opinion here: we are now on the point of law, and must determine according to it; and I know not of any law now in being which will admit of the testimony of an apparition; nor yet, if he did, doth the ghost appear to give evidence.

Crier,' said he, 'call the ghost;' which was done thrice to no manner of purpose: it appeared not.

'Gentlemen of the Jury,' continued the Judge, 'the prisoner at the bar, as you heard, by undeniable witnesses, is a man of most unblemished character; nor hath it appeared, in the course of the examination, that there was any manner of quarrel or grudge between him and the party deceased. I do verily believe him to be perfectly innocent; and, as there is no evidence against him, either positive or circumstantial, he must be acquitted. But from many circumstances which have arisen during the trial, I do strongly suspect that the gentleman who saw the ghost was himself the murderer; in which case he might easily ascertain the pit, the stabs, &c. without any supernatural assistance; and on each suspicion, I shall think myself justified in committing to close custody till the matter can be further inquired into.' This was immediately done, and a warrant granted for searching his house, when such strong proofs of guilt appeared against him, that he confessed the murder, and was executed at the next assize.

The Apparitions Of Portnedown Bridge, Seen
After The Irish Massacre; Being Copies Of The
Evidence Produced By Sir John Temple

1. James Shaw, of Market Hill, in the county Armagh, innkeeper, deposeth, that many of the Irish rebels, in the time of this deponent's restraint, and staying among them, told him very often, and it was a common report, that all those who lived about the bridge of Portnedown were so affrighted with the cries and noises made there of spirit or visions for revenge, as that they durst not stay, but fled away thence, so as they protested, affrighted, to Market Hill, saying, they durst not return thither for fear of those cries and spirits, but took grounds and made (creaghs), in or near the parish of Mulabrac.

Sworn, August 14, 1642.

2. Joan, the relict of Gabriel Constable, late of Durmant, in the county of Armagh, gent. deposeth and saith, that she often heard the rebels, Owen O'Farren, Patrick O'Connellan, and divers others of the rebels at Durmant, earnestly say, protest, and tell one another, that the blood of some of those that were knocked on the head and after-wards drowned at Portnedown bridges, still remained on the bridge and would not be washed away; and that often there appeared visions and apparitions, sometimes of men, sometimes of women, breast high above the water, at or near Portnedown, which did most extremely and fear-fully screech and cry out for vengeance against the Irish that had murdered their bodies there: and that their cries and screeches did so terrify the Irish thereabouts, that none durst stay nor live longer there, but fled and removed

farther into the country, and this was common report amongst the rebels there; and that it passed for a truth amongst them, for any thing she could ever observe to the contrary.

Sworn, January 1, 1643.

3. Catherine, the relict of William Coke, late of the county of Armagh, carpenter, sworn and examined, saith that, about the twentieth of December, 1641, a great number of rebels, in the county, did most barbarously drown at the river, at the bridge of Portnedown; and that, about nine days afterwards, she saw a vision or spirit, in the shape of a man, as she apprehended, that appeared in that river, in the place of the drowning, bolt upright, heart high, with hands lifted up, and stood in that place there, until the latter end of Lent next following; about which time some of the English army, marching in those parts, whereof her husband was one (as he and they confidently affirmed to the deponent), saw that vision or spirit standing upright in the posture aforementioned; but, after that time, the said spirit or vision vanished, and appeared no more that she knoweth. And she heard, but saw not, that there were other visions and apparitions, and much screeching and strange noises heard in that river at times afterwards.

Sworn, February 24, 1643.

4. Elizabeth, the wife of Captain Rice Price, of Armagh, deposeth and saith that she and other women, whose husbands were murdered, hearing of divers apparitions and visions that were seen near Portnedown bridge, since the drowning of her children and the rest of the Protestants there, went unto the aforesaid bridge about twilight in

the evening: there appeared unto them, upon a sudden, a vision or spirit, assuming the shape of a woman, waist-high, upright in the water, naked, with elevated and closed hands, her hair hanging down very white, her eyes seemed to twinkle, and her skin as white as snow; which spirit seemed to stand straight up in the water, and often repeated the words, 'Revenge, revenge, revenge!' whereat this deponent and the rest, being put into a strong amazement, and affrighted, walked from the place.

Sworn, January 29, 1642.

5. Arthur Azlum, of Clowargher, in the county of Cavan, esquire, deposeth, that he was credibly informed by some that were present there, that there were thirty women and young children, and seven men, flung into the river of Belturbet; and, when some of them offered to swim for their lives, they were by the rebels followed in carts, and knocked upon the head with poles. The same day they hanged two women in Turbet: and this deponent doth verily believe that Rutmore O'Reby, the then sheriff, had a hand in commanding the murder of those said persons; for he saw him write two notes, which he sent to Turbet by Brian O'Reby, upon whose coming their murders were committed: and those persons who were present also affirmed that the bodies of those thirty persons drowned did not appear upon the water till about six weeks past; as the said Reby came to the town, all the bodies came floating up to the very bridge; and those persons were all formerly stayed in the town by his protection, when the rest of their neighbours in the town went away.

Apparition Seen By Lord Lyttelton

There have been two Lord Lytteltons, both of whom were marked and distinguished men in their respective generations – the great and good Lord Lyttelton, and his son, the witty and profligate, who is the hero of the present narrative.

Lord Lyttelton, in the winter of the year 1778, had retired from the metropolis, with a party of his loose and dissipated companions, to profane the Christmas by their riotous debaucheries, at his country house, Pit Place, near Epsom, in Surrey. They had not long abandoned themselves to the indulgence of these desperate orgies, when a sudden and unexpected gloom was cast over the party by the extraordinary depression of spirits and dejection of countenance which were observed to take possession of their host; all his vivacity had departed – he fled from the society which he had so solicitously collected around him; his laugh became forced; his eye was fixed upon the ground, and his attention always wandering from the present topic of conversation or amusement; his mind was occupied with a subject that distressed it. It was in vain that he attempted to silence the enquiries of the guests on the subject of his uneasiness: they were convinced that he was ill, or had met some loss at play, or was crossed in love; and his denial of all these imputations only excited a more eager curiosity to be informed of the real origin of his depression. Thus urged, he at last determined to reveal the secret that so painfully distressed him.

The night before, on retiring to his bed, after his servant was dismissed and his light extinguished, he had heard a noise resembling the fluttering of a dove at his chamber window. This attracted his attention to the spot; when, looking in the direction of the sound, he saw the figure of an unhappy female, whom he had seduced and deserted, and who, when deserted, had put a violent end to her own existence, standing in the aperture of the window from which the fluttering sound had proceeded. The form approached the foot of the bed:– the room was preternaturally light; the objects of the chamber were distinctly visible:– raising her hand, and pointing to a dial which stood on the mantelpiece of the chimney, the figure, with a severe solemnity of voice and manner, announced to the appalled and conscience-stricken man, that, at that very hour, on the third day after the visitation, his life and his sins would be concluded, and nothing but their punishment remain if he availed himself not of the warning to repentance which he had received. The eye of Lord Lyttelton glanced on the dial; the hand was on the stroke of twelve:– again the apartment was involved in total darkness:– the warning spirit disappeared, and bore away at her departure all the lightness of heart and buoyancy of spirit, ready flow of wit, and vivacity of manner, which had formerly been the pride and ornament of the unhappy being to whom she had delivered her tremendous summons.

Such was the tale Lord Lyttelton delivered to his companions: they laughed at his superstition, and endeavoured to convince him that his mind must have been impressed with this idea by some dream of a more consistent nature than dreams generally are, and that he had mistaken the visions of his sleep for the visitations of a spirit. He was counselled, but not convinced: he felt relieved by their distrust, and on the second night after the appearance of the spectre, he retreated to his apartment with his faith in the reality of the spectre somewhat shaken; and his spirits, though not relieved, certainly lighted of somewhat of their oppression.

On the succeeding day the guests of Lord Lyttelton, with the connivance of his attendant, had provided that the clocks throughout the house should be advanced an hour and a half: by occupying their host's attention during the whole day with different and successive objects of amusement, they contributed to prevent his discovering the imposture. Ten o'clock struck; the noblemen was silent and depressed: eleven struck; the depression deepened, and now not even a smile, or the slightest movement of his eye indicated him to be conscious of the efforts of his associates, as they attempted to dispel his gloom:– twelve struck:'Thank God! I'm safe,' exclaimed Lord Lyttelton:'The ghost was a liar, after all: some wine, there:– congratulate me, my friends – congratulate me on my reprieve:– why, what a fool I was to be cast down by so silly and absurd a circumstance!– But, however, it's time for bed:– we'll be up early, and out with the hounds to-morrow:– by my faith, it's half-past twelve; so good night, good night:' and he returned to his chamber, convinced of his security, and believing that the threatened hour of peril was now past.

His guests remained together to await the completion of the time so ominously designated by the vision. A quarter of an hour elapsed:– they heard the valet descend from his master's room– it was just twelve:– Lord Lyttelton's bell rang violently:– the company ran in a body to his apartment;– the clock struck one at their entrance (it had been advanced an hour; and it was, in fact, but twelve, the hour intimated by the spectre):– the unhappy nobleman lay extended on the bed before them, pale and lifeless, and his countenance terribly convulsed.

This is the account which the narrator received from a lady, a relation of Lord Lyttelton's: the subsequent passage is from Sir Nathaniel Wraxhall: 'Dining at Pit Place, about four years after the death of Lord Lyttelton, in year 1783, I had the curiosity to visit the bed-chamber, where the casement window, at which Lord Lyttelton asserted the dove appeared to flutter, was pointed out to me; and, at his stepmother's, the dowager Lady Lyttelton's in Portugal Street, Grosvenor Square, who, being a woman of very lively imagination, lent an implicit faith, to all the supernatural facts which were supposed to have accompanied or produced Lord Lyttelton's end, I have frequently seen a painting which she herself executed, in 1780, expressly to commemorate the event: it hung in a conspicuous part of her drawing room. There the dove appears at the window, while a female figure, habited in white, stands at the foot of the bed, announcing to Lord Lyttelton his dissolution.

Every part of the picture was faithfully designed, after the description given to her by the valet-de-chambre who attended him, to whom his master related all the circumstances.'

The Murder Of The Duke Of Buckingham Foretold By His Father's Apparition

An officer in the king's wardrobe, in Windsor Castle (as mentioned in the Earl of Clarendon's History of the Grand Rebellion) an honest and discreet person, about fifty years of age, when he was a school boy, was much taken notice of by Sir George Villiers, the Duke of Buckingham's father, who laid several obligations to him.

This gentleman, as he was lying in bed, perfectly awake, and in very good health, perceived a venerable aspect draw his curtains, and with his eyes fixed upon him, asked him, if he knew who he was? The poor gentleman, after the repetition of the same question, recalling to his memory the presence of Sir George Villiers, answered, half dead with fear, he thought him to be that person. He replied, that he was in the right, and that he must go and acquaint his son from him, 'That unless he did something to ingratiate himself with the people, he would be cut off in a short time.'

After this he disappeared; and the poor man next morning considered all no otherwise than a dream.

This was repeated, with a more terrible aspect the next night, the apparition telling him, 'Unless he performed his commands, he must expect no peace of mind'; upon which he promised to obey him. The lively representation of all to his memory strangely perplexed him: but considering that he was a person at such a distance from the duke, he was still willing to persuade himself that he had been only dreaming.

The same spectre after a repetition of his former threats repeated a third time, and 'reproaching him with breach of promise;' he had by this time got courage to tell him, that it was difficult thing to gain admission to the duke, and more difficult to be credited by him; that he should be looked upon as a malcontent or a madman, and so be sure to be ruined.

The spectre after a repetition of his former threats, replied 'that the duke was known to be of very easy access; that two or three particulars he would and did tell him, and which he charged him never to mention to another person, would give him credit.' And do he repeated his threats and left him.

This apparition so far confirmed the old man, that he repaired to London, where the court then was; and being known to Sir Ralph Freeman who had married a lady nearly allied with the duke, he acquainted him with enough to let him know there was something extraordinary in it, without imparting to him all the particulars.

Sir Ralph having informed the duke of what the man desired, and of all he knew in the matter, his grace according to usual condescension told him, that the next day he was to hunt with the king, that he would land at Lambeth bridge by five in the morning, where, if the person attended, he would talk with him as long as should be necessary: accordingly the man, being conducted by Sir Ralph, met the duke, and walked aside in conference with him near an hour; Sir Ralph, and his servants being at such a distance, that they could not learn a word, though the duke was observed to speak sometimes, and that with great emotion.

The man told Sir Ralph, in his return over the water, that when he mentioned credentials, the substance of which, he said, he was to impart to no man, 'The duke swore he could come to that knowledge by none but the devil; for those particulars were a secret to all but himself and another, who he was sure would never speak of it.'

The duke returned from hunting before the morning was spent, and was shut with his mother for the space of two or three hours in her apartments at Whitehall; and when he left her, his countenance appeared full of trouble with a mixture of anger: and she herself, when the news of the duke's murder was brought to her (his grace being stabbed by one John Felton, a discontented lieutenant, when he was equipping a fleet for the relief of Rochelle, at Portsmouth, on the 23rd day of August, 1628,) seemed to receive it without the least surprise, and as a thing she had long foreseen.

Some time before his death, the duke had been advised by Sir Clement Throgmorton to wear a privy coat; the duke took his counsel very kindly, but gave him this answer: 'that he thought a coat of mail would signify little in a popular commotion, and from any single person he apprehended no danger.'

Notices of Approaching Death

In 1727-8, in the month of February, at which time Langford Collin, Esq. lived at York, one night coming home, he immediately and very speedily undressed himself and went to bed to his lady, who being awake, he spoke to her; but he had hardly exchanged six words when he was surprised at a sudden knock given to the street-door, so loud, as if it had been a great sledge hammer, which made him as suddenly rise up out of his bed, and with a pair of pistols in his hands, he hasted across to the dining room, but before he could reach the door of it, he heard a second knock, full as loud as the first; at which impatient, and fearing it might injure his lady then pregnant, and near her time, he with all expedition did run to the window, during which a third knock was heard, not only by himself, but several of his family; but throwing the sash open, he saw nobody, neither at the door, nor on one side or other of the house, though it was clear moon-light, and nothing to obstruct his sight either way for a considerable space.

Still thinking it was done by some unlucky persons out of game or wantonness, he discovered next morning his uneasiness at such usage, at the coffee-house, declaring with some warmth how highly he would resent it, could he come to the knowledge of the rude person who had been guilty of the ridiculous action; nor did he change his first opinion till the next post bought him a letter, which informed him of the death of his cousin, Thomas Smith, Esq. of Nottingham, who died at London at the time the said knocking was heard.

About three years after that, the same gentleman sitting up with his next brother, Mr Abel Collin, heard from twelve o'clock at night till it struck one, a continual noise of driving nails into a coffin, in the workshop of John Baker, a joiner, which abutted onto their yard; at this he was very much offended, as thinking it very unkind from an intimate acquaintance of a sick person, when soon after he heard a noise as if two or three men were landing a coffin in the room over his head, which made him suspect it to be a fore-runner of his brother's death, who departed this life exactly at one o'clock the next day.

Extraordinary Predictions

The fame of Theresa Sensari was universal in November, 1774. She was in appearance a gentlewoman of about sixty years of age, a church going devotee, and a widow, of a small, though sufficient fortune, had no family but one woman servant. This gentlewoman foretold, or rather prophesied, (for they called her a prophetess), that the late kings of Sardinia and France, likewise the late Pope, should die at the three different periods of time which she marked down; and told every body with frankness the day that each should die. At first when she propagated this strange story, people looked upon her as a mad woman, and ridiculed her in every company, (for she visited several genteel families), but, when the king of Sardinia died the day she had fore- told, people began to give credit to her prophecy.

Cardinal Albani, in a jocular way, told this to the late Pope, and his holiness laughed it off with the cardinal. This woman still persisted that the king of France would die on the day that she had mentioned, and which to the astonish- ment of every body, happened on the very day; for she had said to several persons, 'the king of France will die to-day'. Several persons took notice of this, and were in great expec- tation for the French post, to know the truth of it, when to their great surprise, they found it true: this made a great noise, particularly at Rome. Cardinal Albini then sent his coach to fetch her; she would not accept of his coach, but immediately came on foot.

The cardinal asked her whether it was true that she had foretold such strange things. She replied in the affirmative. 'Pray, madam,' said the cardinal, 'how came you to know such things, for it is incomprehensible to me how you should tell such events?' 'Wonder not, my lord,' said she, 'for God knows every thing, and it is from him alone that I know it.' Though the cardinal argued a long time with her, he could get no other answer than the above. The cardinal went immediately to the pope; and acquainted him with every particular, when his holiness desired to speak with her. She went immediately, and the pope took her gently by the hand, and said, 'my blessing on thee, honest woman; I am told that you have the knowledge of future events, and that you have foretold the deaths of the king of Sardinia, the king of France, and mine; and the two first you have guessed right at.' 'May it please your holiness, it was no guess, but I am as sure of it as I am here, for God told me precisely to a day.' 'Good woman,' said the pope, still holding her by the hand, 'I must not be put off with such stories; I declare before my friends here, that I will do you no manner of harm; nay, I will reward you, if you will tell me the truth.' To which she answered, 'may it please your holiness, I have told you nothing but the truth, so help me God.'

The pope then said, dropping her hand, 'is that all you have got to say for yourself?' 'That's all,' said she, 'and your holiness may rest assured it will be as God told me.' 'Well then, good woman, you shall go, and remain in prison till then; we shall know whether you are a good or a bad prophetess.' The pope then ordered her to be imprisoned in the castle of St Angelo. She was not in the least dismayed at her sentence, and when coming out of the room she only said, 'God's will be done.' The pope gave orders that proper care should be taken of her, and to let her want for nothing. She was visited by vast numbers of people of every denomination, and they never heard her complain of her situation, she preserving the same tranquillity she ever did, and still persisting in her former story.

The pope died the very day she foretold.

She had often been asked by ladies and gentlemen at divers times, whether she could foretell when she would be released; and she said, 'No; God hath not told me yet.' She always bore a very good character; there were people at Rome who had known her from her infancy, and that she was looked upon as a just, modest, and religious woman. Strange as this story may appear, yet it was corroborated by a number of letters from several parts of Italy, and they all agreed, and confirmed the same.

Persons Supposed Dead Returned To Life

A shoemaker's wife in the parish of Cripplegate, being thought dead, was, agreeable to her desire, buried in her wedding cloaths; her ring being on her finger, induced the sexton to open the grave in the night, in order to steal it; when finding it not easy to come off, he took his knife to cut the finger from the hand; which operation recalled the woman to her senses, and she rose from her coffin. The affrighted villain took to his heels; and she, taking his lanthorn, walked home, knocked up her husband, and lived several years after. Her monument is yet standing in Cripplegate-church.

That is wonderful which befell two brothers, knights at Rome; the elder of whom was named Corfidius, who being in the repute of all men dead, the tablets of his last will and testament were recited, in which he made his brother the heir of all he had: but in the midst of the funeral preparations, he rose with great cheerfulness upon his legs, and said 'that he had been with his brother, who had recommended the care of his daughter unto him, and had also shewed him where he had hid a great quantity of gold under the ground, wherewith he should defray the funeral expenses.' While he was speaking in this manner, to the admiration of all that were present, a messenger came with the news of his brother's death; and the gold was also found in the very place he had said.

'There was,' saith Gregorious, 'one Raparatus, a Roman, who being stiff and cold, was given over by his relations, as one who was undoubtedly dead; when soon after he returned to life, and sent a messenger to the shrine of St Laurence in Rome, in inquire concerning Tiburtius the priest there, if any thing had befallen him. In the meantime, while the messenger was gone, he told them that were with him, that he had seen Tiburtius tormented in hell with terrible flames. The messenger he had sent returned with this news, that Tiburtius had departed this life; and soon after Raparatus himself died.'

Everardus Ambula, a German knight, fell sick in Germany, in the time of Pope Innocent the Third; and when he had lain for some time as one dead, returning to himself, he said, that his soul was carried by evil spirits into the city of Jerusalem, thence into the camp of Saladine, who then reigned in Egypt, from thence it was conveyed to Lombardy, where he had spoken to a friend of his: lastly, he was brought to the city of Rome, the situation, the form of the palaces and buildings of which, together with the features of divers princes there, he most exactly described as they were: and although this is a matter of admiration, yet the greater wonder is, that he, with whom he said he did converse in the wood, affirmed that he was there, at the same time and hour, discoursed with this Everardus, according as he had declared.

Acilius Aviola was concluded dead, both by his domestics and physicians; accordingly he was laid out upon the ground for some time, and then carried forth to his funeral fire: but as soon as the flames began to catch his body, he cried out that he was alive, imploring the assistance of his school-master, who was the only person who had tarried with him; but it was too late, for, encompassed with flames, he was dead before he could be succoured.

Sucius Lamias had been praetor, and being supposed to be dead, he was carried, after the Roman manner, to be burnt; being surrounded with the flames, he cried out that he lived; but in vain, for he could not be withdrawn from his fate.

Plato tells us of Erus Amenius being slain in battle, among many others; when they came to take up the dead bodies on the tenth day after, they found that, though all the other carcases were putrid, this of his was entire and uncorrupted; they therefore carried it home, that it might have the just and due funeral rites performed. Two days they kept it in that state, and on the twelfth he was taken out to the funeral pile; and being ready to be laid on it, he returned to life, to the admiration of all that were present. He declared several strange and prodigious things, which he had seen and known during all that time that he remained in the state of the dead.

One of the noble family of the Tatoriedi, being seized with the plague in Burgundy, was supposed to die thereof, and was put into a coffin to be carried to the sepulchre of his ancestors, which was distant some four German miles from that place. Night coming on, the corpse was disposed of in a barn, and there attended by some rustics. These perceived a great quantity of fresh blood to issue through the chinks of the coffin; whereupon they opened it, and found that the body was wounded by a nail that was driven into the shoulder through the coffin; and that the wound was much torn by the jogging of the chariot he was carried in: but that withal they discovered that the natural heat had not left his breast. They took him out, and laid him before a fire; he recovered as out of a deep sleep, ignorant of all that had passed. He afterwards married a wife, by whom he had a daughter, married afterwards to Huldericus a Psirt; from his daughter came Sagismundus a Psirt, chief pastor of Saint Mary's church in Basil.

In 1658, Elizabeth, the servant of one Mrs Cope, of Magdalen College, Oxford, was convicted of killing her bastard child, and was accordingly hanged at Green Ditch, where she hung so long that one of the by-standers said, if she was not dead, he would be hanged for her. When cut down, the gallows being very high, she fell with such violence to the ground, that the concussion seemed sufficient of itself to have killed her. After this she was put into a coffin, and carried to the George inn, in Magdalen parish; where signs of life being observed in her, she was blooded, and put to bed with a young woman; by which means she came to herself, and, to all appearance, might have lived many years; but the next night, she was, by the order of one Mallory, a bailiff of the city, barbarously dragged to

Tales from the Terrific Register

Gloucester Green, and there hanged upon the arm of a tree till she was dead.

Exorcising

Sir Eyles Irwin in his voyage up the Red Sea observes that, besides our nokidah and pilot, there was another Arab on board: the rest of the crew were Abyssinians. During the first watch at night, which it was my turn to keep, this Arab, who was talking to his companions, suddenly fell upon the deck in the stern of the boat, and to all appearance, was seized with a convulsive fit. We were immediately in motion, and offered to administer such relief to him, as we had seen practised in the same cases. But our astonishment was great, when we found the Arabs would not permit any assistance to be given him. They declared that he was only disordered in mind, and that an evil spirit possessed him, who could only be expelled by the force of prayer. Accordingly the nokidah began to pray over him aloud, while two men held the unhappy creature down, to prevent, as they said, the ill effects of the temporary influence which over-ruled him. They told us stories of men in this situation, who committed murder, and every other act of desperation. This idea seemed so extravagant to us, that we treated it with ridicule; and could not but pity the ignorance of a people, who were such slaves to superstition. The notion was certainly imbibed from the demoniacs of Palestine, who are mentioned in the New Testament. We were much surprised, however, at the length of the fit, which continued between two or three hours; and, from the strong agitations of his body, left the Arab in a state of imbecility for the rest of the night. But the devil was at length exorcised, and the nokidah remarked to us with triumph, the great efficacy of prayer!

An Account Of An Apparition

SIR,   Dec. 15th, 1697

...I have sent you inclosed a relation of an apparition; the story I had from two persons, who each had it from the author, and yet their accounts somewhat varied, and passing through more mouths, has varied much more; therefore, I got a friend to bring me the author's, at a chamber, where I wrote it down from the author's own mouth, after which I read it to him, and gave him another copy; he said he could swear to the truth of it as far as he is concerned: he is the curate of Warblington, bachelor of arts, of Trinity College, in Oxford, about six years standing in the University; I hear no ill report of his behaviour here, he is now gone to his curacy; he has promised to send up the hand writing of the tenant and his man, who is a smith by trade, and the farmer's man, as far as they are concerned. Mr Brereton, the rector, would have him say nothing of the story, for that he can get no tenant, though he has offered the house for ten pounds a year less. Mr P. the former incumbent, whom the apparition represented, was a man of very ill report, supposed to have had children by his maid, and to have murdered them; but I advised the curate to say nothing himself of this last part of P. but leave that to the parishioners who knew him. Those who knew this P. said he had exactly such a gown, and that he used to whistle. Yours,   J. CASSWELL.

'At Warblington near Havant, in Hampshire, within six miles of Portsmouth, in the parsonage house dwelt Thomas Perch the tenant, with his wife and a child, a man servant Thomas ———, and a maid servant. About the beginning of August anno, 1695, on a Monday about nine or ten at night, all being gone to bed except the maid with the child; the maid being in the kitchen, and having raked up the fire, took a candle in one hand, and the child in the other arm, and turning about, saw some one in a black gown walking through the room, and thence out of the door into the orchard: upon this the maid, hasting, having recovered but two steps, cried out; on which the master and mistress ran down, found the candle in her hand, she grasping the child about its neck with the other arm; she told them the reason of her crying out. She would not tarry that night in the house, but removed to another belonging to one Henry Salter, farmer; where she cried out all night from the terror she was in, and she could not be persuaded to go any more into the house upon any terms.

On the morrow, the tenant's wife came to my lodging, then at Havant, to desire my advice, and to have a consultation with some friends about it. I told her that I thought it was a flam, and that they had a mind to abuse Mr Brereton the rector, whose house it was; she desired me to come up; I told her I would come up, and sit up, or lie there, as she pleased; for then as to all stories of ghosts and apparitions, I was an infidel: I went thither, and sat up

on the Tuesday night with the tenant and his man servant: about twelve or one o'clock I searched all the rooms
in the house to see if any body was hid there to impose
upon me. We went down into the kitchen where we were
before, and sat up there the remaining part of the night
and had no manner of disturbance.

Thursday night the tenant and I lay together in one room,
and the man in another, and he saw something walk along
in a black gown, and place itself against a window, and there
stood for some time and then walked off. Friday morning
he related this. I asked him why he did not call me, and
told him I thought that was a trick or flam; he told me the
reason why he did not call me, was that he was not able to
speak or move. Friday night we lay as before, and Saturday
night, and had no disturbance either of the nights.

Sunday night I lay by myself in one room (not that where
the man saw the apparition) and the tenant and his man in
another; and between twelve and two the man heard something walk in the room at the bed's feet, and whistling very
well; at last it came to the bed's side, drew the curtain, and
looked on them; after some time it moved off; then the man
called to me, desired me to come, for there was something
in the room went about whistling: I asked whether he had
any light or could strike one: he told me no; then I leaped
out of bed and not staying to put on my clothes, went out
of my room and along a gallery to the door, which I found
locked or bolted; I desired him to unlock the door, for that
I could not get in; then he got out of bed and opened the
door which was near, and went immediately to bed again;
I went in three or four steps, and it being a moon-shine
night, I saw the apparition move from the bed-side, and
clap up against the wall that divided their room and mine;

I went and stood directly against it, and asked in the name of God what it was made it come disturbing us; I stood some time expecting an answer, and receiving none, and thinking it might be some fellow hid in a room to frighten me, I put out my hand to feel it, and my hand went seemingly through the body of it and felt no manner of substance, till it came to the wall: then I drew back my hand and still it was in the same place.

Till now I had not the least fear, and even now very little; then I adjured it to tell me what it was: when I said these words, it, keeping its back against the wall, moved gently along towards the door; I followed it, and it going out of the door turned its back towards me; I went a little into the gallery, and it disappeared where there was no corner for it to turn to, and before it came to the end of the gallery, where was the stairs. Then I found myself very cold from my feet as high as my middle, though I was not in great fear; I went into bed between the tenant and his man and they complained of my being exceedingly cold. The tenant's man leaned over his master in the bed, and saw me stretch out my hand towards the apparition, and heard me speak the words; the tenant also heard the words. The apparition seemed to have a morning gown of a darkish colour, no hat nor cap, short black hair, a thin meagre visage of a pale swarthy colour, seemed to be about forty-five, or fifty years old; the eyes half shut, the arms hanging down; the hands visible beneath the sleeve; of a middle stature. I related this description to Mr John Larner, rector of Havant parish; they both said, the description agreed very well to Mr P., a former rector of the place, who has been dead above twenty years: upon this the tenant and his wife left the house which has remained void ever since.

The Monday after last Michaelmas day, a man of Chodson in Warwickshire, having been at the Havant fair, passed the aforesaid parsonage house about nine or ten at night, and saw a light in most rooms of the house; his pathway being close by the house, he wondering at the light looked into the kitchen windows, and saw only a light, but turning himself to go away, he saw the appearance of a man in a long gown; he made haste away; the apparition followed him over a piece of glebe land of several acres, to a lane which he crossed, and over a little meadow, then over another lane to some pales, which belonged to farmer Henry Salter, my landlord, near a barn, in which were some of the farmer's men, and some others; this man went into the barn, told them how he was frightened and followed from the parsonage by an apparition, which they may see standing against the pales if they went out: they went out and saw it scratch against the pales, and make a hideous noise; it stood there some time, and then disappeared; their descriptions agreed with what I saw. This last account I had from the man himself whom it followed, and also from the farmer's men.

Friendship After Life

Caesar Baronius tells, that there was an entire friendship betwixt Michael Mercatus the elder, and Marsilius Ficinus; and this friendship was the stronger betwixt them, by reason of a mutual agreement in their studies, and an equal veneration for the doctrines of Plato. It fell out that these two discoursed together (as they used) of the state of man after death, according to Plato's opinions; but when their disputation and discourse was drawn out somewhat long, they shut it up with this firm agreement, 'That whichsoever of the two should first depart out of this life, if possible, should ascertain the survivor of the state of the other life, and whether the soul be immortal or not.'

Some time after this agreement was made, it fell out, that while Michael Mercatus was one morning early at his study, upon a sudden he heard the noise of a horse upon the gallop, and then stopping at his door; withal he heard the voice of Marsilius his friend, crying to him, 'O Michael, Michael! those things are true, they are true!' Michael wondering to hear his friend's voice, rose up, and opening the casement, he saw the back of him whom he had heard, in white, and galloping away upon a white horse. He called after him, 'Marsilius, Marsilius!' and followed him with his eye. But he soon vanished out of his sight. He, amazed at this extraordinary accident, very solicitously inquired, if any thing had happened to Marsilius (who then lived in France, where he also breathed his last), and he found, upon strict inquiry, that he died at that very time, wherein he was thus heard and seen by him.

Prediction Of A Spirit

Ludovicus Adolisius, lord of Immola, sent a secretary of his upon earnest business to Ferrara; in which journey he was met by one on horseback, attired like a huntsman, with a hawk upon his fist, who saluted him by his name, and desired him to intreat his son Lodowick to meet him in that very place the next day, at the same hour, to whom he would discover certain things of no mean importance, which much concerned him and his estate.

The secretary returning and revealing this to his lord; at first he would scarce give credit to his report, and jealous withal that it might be some train laid to entrap his life, he sent another in his stead: to whom the same spirit appeared in the shape aforesaid, and seemed to lament his son's diffidence; to whom, if he had come in person, he would have related strange things, which threatened his estate, and the means how to prevent them. Yet desired him to recommend him to his son, and tell him, that after twenty-two years, one month and one day, prefixed, he should lose the government of that city, which he then possessed, and so he vanished. It happened just at the time the spirit had predicted (notwithstanding his great care and providence) that Philip, duke of Milan, the same night besieged the city, and by the help of the ice (it being then a sharp frost) passed the moat, and with scaling ladders, scaled the wall, surprised the city, and took Ludowick prisoner. He was in league with Philip, and therefore feared no harm from him.

Coming To Life

Colonel Townsend, a gentleman of honour and integrity, had for many years been afflicted with a nephritic complaint. His illness increasing, and his strength decaying, he came from Bristol to Bath, in a litter, in autumn, and lay at the Bell inn. Dr Baynard and I (Dr Cheyne) were called to him, and attended him twice a day, but his vomiting continuing still incessant and obstinate against all remedies; we despaired of his recovery. While he was in this condition, he sent for us one morning; we waited on him, with Mr Skine, his apothecary. We found his senses clear, and his mind calm: his nurse and several servants were about him. He told us, he had sent for us, to give us an account of an odd sensation he had for some time observed and felt in himself; which was, that, composing himself, he could die or expire when he pleased, and yet by an effort, or some how, he could come to life again; which he had sometimes tried before he sent for us.

We heard this with surprise; but as it was not to be accounted for from common principles, we could hardly believe the fact as he related it, much less give an account of it; unless he should please to make the experiment before us, which we were unwilling he should do, lest in his weak condition, he might carry it too far. He continued to talk very distinctly and sensibly, above a quarter of an hour about this surprising affliction, and insisted so much on our seeing the trial made, that we were at last forced to comply. We all three felt his pulse first; it was distinct, though small and thready; and his heart had its usual beating. He composed himself on his back, and lay in a still posture for some time; while I held his right hand, Dr Baynard laid his hand on his heart, and Mr Skrine held a clean looking-glass to his mouth. I found his pulse sink gradually, till at last I could not feel any, by the most exact and nice touch. Dr Baynard could not feel the least motion in his heart, nor Mr Skine the least soil of breath on the bright mirror he held to his mouth: then each of us, by turns, examined his arm, heart, and breath, but could not, by the nicest scrutiny, discover the least symptom of life in him. We reasoned a long time about this odd appearance as well as we could, and all of us judging it inexplicable and unaccountable, and finding he still continued in that condition, we began to conclude that he had indeed carried the experiment too far, and at last were satisfied that he was actually dead, and were just ready to leave him.

This continued about half an hour. As we were going away, we observed some motion about his body, and, upon examination, found his pulse and the motion of his heart gradually returning: he began to breathe gently, and speak softly: we were all astonished to the last degree at this unexpected change, and after some further conversation with him, and amongst ourselves, went away fully satisfied as to all the particulars of this fact, but confounded and puzzled, and not able to form any rational scheme that might account for it. He afterwards called for his attorney, added a codicil to his will, settled legacies on his servants, received the sacrament, and calmly and composedly expired, between five and six o'clock that evening.

Next day he was opened (as he had ordered); his body was the soundest and best made I had ever seen; his lungs were fair, large, and sound, his heart big and strong, and his intestines sweet and clean; his stomach was of a due proportion, the coat sound and thick, and the vallous member entire. But when we came to examine the kidneys, though the left was sound and of a just size, the right was about four times as big, distended like a blown bladder, and yielding as if full of pap; he having often passed a weyish liquor during his illness. Upon opening the kidney we found it quite full of white chalky matter, like plaister of Paris, and all the fleshy substance dissolved and worn away, by what I called a nephritic cancer. This had been the source of all his misery; and the symptomatic vomitings from the irritation of the consentient nerves, had quite starved and worn him down. I have narrated the facts as I saw and observed them deliberately and distinctly, and shall leave to the philosophic reader to make what inference he thinks fit; the truth of the material circumstances I will warrant.

Dreams And Presentiments

As the king, Henry IV of France, was accompanying the queen into his cabinet, he stopped to speak to somebody, upon which the queen stopped also, 'Passez, passez, Madame la Regente,' i.e. 'Go on, go on, Madam the Regent,' said the king. A few days before his death the queen had two odd dreams. She fancied that the diamonds, rubies, and other jewels in her crown, were changed into pearls, and that she was told pearls signified tears. The night after she started and cried out in her sleep; the king waking, caught her in his arms, and asked her what was the matter. 'I have had a frightful dream,' said she, 'but dreams are delusions.' 'I have always thought so too,' said the king; 'however, tell me what it was.' With much entreaty she proceeded. 'I dreamt,' said she, 'that you were stabbed with a knife under the short ribs.' 'Blessed be God,' said the king, 'it was but a dream,' and so went to sleep.

On the day the king was killed, he was observed to be very uneasy; nay, he observed it himself, and said several times, that something sat heavy on his heart. When he was going out he asked if the coach was below. The villain who killed him was at the foot of the stairs, and was heard to mutter, 'I have you, you are lost.' He thrice took leave of the queen before he went into the coach. He seemed then to resume himself, he forbad the guards to follow him out of the Louvre; sent the captain to Palais; the lieutenant was sick; the ensign was gone with a message to the President du Harlay; so that the coach was open on all sides; his attendants went through another street; the Rue de la Ferronneire being very narrow, was encumbered with two wagons, one laden with wine, the other with corn, which obliged the king's coach to stop. At that instant the king threw back his cloak, and put himself in such a position, as left his left side wholly exposed to the assassin, who said himself afterwards, that he thrust his knife into the king's body, as into a sack of corn.

Neglected Warning

James IV King of Scotland, being persuaded by the clergy and bishops to break with England, and declare war against Henry VIII, contrary to the advice of his nobility and gentry, who were to bear both the expense and the blows of a battle; the king, thus overruled by the clergy, raised an army and prepared to march to the frontiers: but the evening before he was to take the field, as he was at vespers in the chapel royal at his palace of Linlithgow, an ancient man appeared to him with a long head of hair the colour of amber, (some accounts represent it as a glory round his head) and of a venerable aspect, having on a belted plaid girt round with a linen sash. This man was perceived by the king before he came up close to him, and before he was seen by any of the people; and the king also perceived him to be earnestly looking at him, and at the noble persons about him, as desiring to speak to him.

After some little time, he pressed through the crowd, and came close up to the king, and, without any reverence or bow made to his person, told him with a low voice, but such as the king could hear distinctly, that he was sent to him to warn him not to proceed in the war which he had undertaken at the solicitation of the priests, and in favour of the French; and that if he did go on with it he should not prosper. He added also, that if he did not abstain from his lewd and unchristian practices with wicked women, they would end in his destruction.

Having delivered this message he immediately vanished; for though his pressing up to the king had put the whole assembly in disorder, and every one's eye was fixed on him when he was delivering his message to the king; yet no one saw him any more, or perceived his going back from the king; which put them all into the utmost consternation.

The king himself was also in great confusion; he would fain have believed that the spectre was a man, and would have spoken to him again, and asked some questions of him. But the people constantly and with one voice affirmed it was an angel and that it immediately disappeared after the message was delivered; that they plainly saw him and felt him thrusting to get by them as he went up, but not one could see him go back. The king upon this was satisfied that it was not a real body, but an apparition; and it put him in great consternation, and caused him to delay his march awhile, and call several councils of his nobility to consider what to do.

But the king still being overpersuaded by those engines employed by Monsieur La Motte, the French ambassador, continued in his designs for a war, and advanced with his army to the Tweed, which was the boundary of the two kingdoms.

Here the army rested some time, and the king being at Jedburgh, a known town in those parts, as he was sitting drinking wine very plentifully in a great hall of the house where his head-quarters was then held, supposed to be the old Earl of Morton's house, the spectre came to him a second time, though not in the form which he appeared at Linlithgow, and with less regard and respect to the prince, and in an imperious tone told him he was commanded to warn him not to proceed in that war, for if he did, he should lose not the battle only, but his crown and kingdom; and after this, without staying for any answer, went to the chimney, and wrote on the stone over it, or that which we call the mantle-piece, the following distich:

Laeta sit illa dies, nescitur origo secundi,
Sit labor an requies, sio transit gloria mundi.

That the king did not listen to either of these notices, our histories, as well as Buchanan, the historian of Scotland, take notice of very publicly; and also that he marched on, fought the English at Flodden Field, and there lost his army, all his former glory, and his life.

Caution Of A Brother's Spirit

Two wealthy merchants travelling through the Taurine hills into France, upon the way they met a man of more than human stature who thus said to them: 'Salute my brother Lewis Sforza, and deliver him this letter from me.' They were amazed, and asked who he was? He told them, that he was Galeacius Sforza, and immediately vanished from sight. They made haste to Milan, and delivered the Duke's letter, wherein was thus written: 'On Lewis! take heed of thyself, for the Venetians and French will unite to thy ruin, and deprive thy posterity of their estate. But if thou wilt deliver me three thousand guilders, I will endeavour that the spirits being reconciled, thy unhappy fate may be averted; and this I hope to perform, if thou shalt not refuse what I have requested: farewell.' This was laughed at by most as a fiction: but not long after, the duke was dispossessed of his government, and taken prisoner by Lewis XII King of France.

The Midnight Assassination

In the county of Galway, in Ireland, there lived a young couple, the children of the two neighbouring cottagers, who were betrothed to each other from the earliest period of infancy. They had been educated in the same rude

retirement, had partaken of the same fare, had shared in the same amusements; and were now anxiously waiting the period of their union. Their parents were of the lowest class of Irish peasantry, and possessed no inconsiderable share of the national virtues and vices. With dispositions naturally good, their passions had been inflamed by the civil dissensions of the period, and embittered by the pressure of acute poverty; and which finally induced them to join the ill-fated rebellion, that terminated in the death of poor Emmett and his associates, [and sadly, also in the death of the young man himself].

It was dusk when the Irishman arrived at his cottage, and the voice of wailing was loud within. He entered, and beheld his wife, with a young woman seated by her side: and his daughter, the child of his pride, dying from positive exigence. After the death of her betrothed husband, she had gradually drooped and bowed her fair head towards the tomb. Life henceforth was a scene of utter solitude; the light that shone on her path had vanished, and darkness encompassed it all around. With a faint smile she held out her hand to her father, and sunk back exhausted on her couch of straw. Unacquainted with the cause of her complaint, he turned to his wife for further information, and was told in reply, that neither herself or her daughter had eaten any thing for the last two days, for that every trifling sum they could procure, had been devoted to medicine for their child. Her countenance darkened as she spoke, and with a ghastly grin of the most diabolical tendency, she drew her husband in silence from the room, and whispered in his ear that the young woman, who at that time lodged in their cottage, had saved up a guinea while at service, and proposed that it should be appropriated to themselves.

After a long struggle between their horror at the idea of murder, and their affection for their child, they resolved to despatch the poor woman, and devote the spoils to the subsistence of themselves and daughter. At the dread hour of midnight they entered the room where the two females reposed on the same miserable truck, and in order to ensure the destruction of their victim, remarked that she was stationed nearest to the door, while their daughter slept contiguous to the cottage wall. Having carefully ascertained this point, they entered in an adjoining apartment, and conversed in an audible tone upon the way in which the murderous scheme should be executed.

In the meantime the young woman, roused by the conversation, and over-hearing the frequent repetition of her name, listened in breathless silence, and but too soon became acquainted with the proposed plan of murder. Not a moment was to be lost: she hastily changed places with her sleeping companion, and crept gently over by the cottage wall, which the parents imagined was the corner that their child occupied. All was now silent, but in a few minutes the door of the room was lifted gently on its latch, and a head was thrust forward. The form advanced, and was succeeded by another, bearing a dark lantern in her hand. They approached the bed in quiet, but in the agitation of their movements the light was extinguished. The young woman continued in the most fearful suspense, and could distinctly hear the sharpening of the murderous weapon, and see its blade glittering in the darkness of the room. In an instant it was drawn across the throat of the victim – it cut with a keen edge, wizzed while it separated the arteries, and the blood welled in a purple tide from the wound. The hollow death-rattle followed, the sinews of the body became contracted with convulsions, and a long deep sigh announced that the midnight murder was effected.

The wretches removed the apparel of their victim into the next apartment, and they returned to commit the corpse to earth. Followed at a slight distance by the young woman, who boldly resolved to track their footsteps, they bore it swiftly from the house, and hastened to the grave that had been dug for its reception. The night was wild and tempestuous, and the thunder reverberated in ten thousand echoes along the murky arch of heaven. The wind howled across the moors, and every succeeding gust spoke of unrelieved horror. Not a star was seen in the firmament, but all grew black and dismal, save where the lightning's flash irradiated the landscape, and betrayed its utter desolation. The guilty couple felt the silent awe of the moment, and as they stole quietly along with their lifeless burden hanging on their arms, listened with renewed affright to each passing whisper of the breeze. They had now reached the extremity of the gardens, and with paralysed hearts cast the corpse into the burial place. It sunk with a heavy sound into the grave, the face was turned upwards, and a sudden flash of lightning, as it shone full on the dead body, revealed the features of their daughter, of that child for whose sake the murder had been committed.

They were roused from their trance of agony by a deep-drawn sigh, and the sound of approaching footsteps; and by the blue flashes of lightning, and the dim light of their lantern, beheld a form clad in white approaching the spot where they were stationed. It proceeded with slow and solemn steps, and when nearly opposite the grave, beckoned them with its hand to follow. The conscience of the murderers instantly took alarm, and suggested to their disordered imagination that it was the ghost of their slaughtered victim. Struck to the soul with the sight, her past guilt rushing full on her mind, the feelings of the mother were unequal to the struggle, she gave one deep heart-rending groan, and dropped dead on the body of her daughter. The father returned in a state of phrenzy to his cottage, was impeached on the evidence of the young woman, who had encountered them at the grave, and was shortly afterwards executed for the murder.

The spot where he lies buried may still be seen, but is now generally avoided as a residence of unholy spirits. It stands at a slight distance from the main road, and is embosomed on one side by a dark wood, and on the other by the bleak moors of Galway. It is known as the grave where the murderer reposes, and the liberal-minded people, when they shudder at the crimes of him who sleeps below, curse in the bitterness of their hearts the apostates who caused such guilt by the miseries they have entailed on their country.

Pentilly House, Cornwall

Mr Tilly, once the owner of Pentilly House, was a celebrated atheist of the last age. He was a man of wit, and had by rote of all the ribaldry and common-place jests against religion and scripture which are well suited to display pertness and folly, and to unsettle the giddy mind, but are offensive to men of sense, whatever their opinions may be, and are neither intended or adapted to investigate truth. In general the witty atheist is satisfied with entertaining his contemporaries; but Mr Tilly wishes to have his sprightliness known to posterity. With this view, in ridicule of the resurrection, he obliged his executors to place his dead body, in his usual garb, and in his elbow chair, upon the top of the hill, and to arrange on a table before him, bottles, glasses, pipes, and tobacco. In this situation, he ordered himself to be immured in a tower of such magnitude and such dimensions as he described, where he proposed, he said, patiently to await the event! All this was done; and the tower, still enclosing its tenant, remains as a monument of his impiety and profaneness.

Polus, The Actor

When this famous tragedian was to play such a part as required to be represented with remarkable passion, he privily brought in the urn and bones of his dead son, whereby he so excited his own passion, and was moved to deliver himself with that efficacy both in words and gesture, that he filled the whole theatre with unfeigned lamentations and tears.

The Modern Magician

The following extraordinary event happened in Lincolnshire, in the autumn of 1807, at least if we may believe the papers of that period, which state it to be an absolute and well authenticated fact.

Sir Henry E. was riding out one day, when from sudden terror or some other accident, his horse startled and flung him with violence to the ground,– with such violence indeed that he lay for a long time insensible. On recovering his senses, he faintly exclaimed, 'Where am I?' and looking up found himself in the arms of a venerable old man, to whose kind offices he was probably indebted for his life. 'I rejoice in your recovery, but as you are yet affected by your fall, allow me to support you to my house, which is

close at hand. A little quiet is absolutely essential to you.'
Sir Henry expressed his grateful acceptance of the proffered
kindness, and, supported by his new acquaintance, walked
slowly towards the house. Here the unremitting attention
of the old man and his servants soon restored his scattered
senses; his limbs, indeed, ached with the fresh bruises, but
he had reason to congratulate himself on coming off with
unbroken bones; at least if he had no great cause to rejoice,
he had still less to complain.

Dinner was now announced, when he was requested
by the kind old host to join the party, a request to which
he acceded as much from curiosity as any other motive.
Hereupon he was shown into a large hall, where sixteen
covers were laid, and every thing was in a style beyond
mere comfort. The party consisted of the same number,
all gentlemen. The old man sat at the head of the table, an
excellent dinner was served up, and the lively conversation,
which seasoned it, soon made Sir Henry forget his accident. If there was any drawback to the general mirth, it was
from the strange temper of the host; this at times showed
itself in a most singular and whimsical exertion of authority,
which, however, seemed to be disputed by none. Thus for
instance, the gentleman on Sir Henry's left hand asked him
to drink a glass of wine, when the host extending his hand,
exclaimed in a dignified and authoritative tone, 'No.' Sir H.,
though astonished at this check, remained silent, not knowing whether he should attribute it to avarice or insolence,
or both united.

The instant dinner was over, the old man left the room,
when the gentleman who had asked Sir H. to take a glass
of wine, addressed him in a tone and manner that surprised
him still more than the conduct of his host. 'By what mis-

fortune, Sir, have you been unhappily trepanned by that unfeeling villain who just now quitted us? Oh, Sir! you will have ample cause to curse the fatal hour that found you in his power, for you will have no prospect in this world but misery and oppression. Perpetually subject to the capricious humour of the old man, you will remain in this mansion for the remainder of your days; your life will become, as mine is, burdensome; and driven to despair, your days will glide on in regret and melancholy, in cold and miserable confinement. This, alas, has been my lot for fifteen years; and not mine only, but the lot of every one you see here since their arrival at this cursed abode.'

Sir Henry was bewildered; there was so much truth of grief depicted in the stranger's face, that he knew not what to think; he could see there was no deceit in his words – and yet how to believe them? It was against reason, it was against common sense to credit a tale so monstrous. Fear and indignation mutually swayed him, as he exclaimed, 'By what authority can any man detain me against my will? I will not submit: I will oppose him by force if necessary.' 'Ah, Sir,' exclaimed a second gentleman, 'your argument is just, but your threats are in vain; the old man is a magician, we know it by fatal experience; do not be rash, Sir; your attempt would prove fatal, and your punishment would be dreadful.' 'I will endeavour to escape,' said Sir Henry, hardly apprehending the singular words of the speaker. 'Impossible,' replied a third, 'such hopes are groundless, as we have all proved by the attempt: it was but six months ago, that in the endeavour to fly from this abominable place, I broke my leg.' Sir Henry was inclined to be incredulous, but all present had something to add in confirmation of the story. One said he had fractured his arm, a second told him how many had been killed in falls in such attempts; a third that others had suddenly disappeared and never since been heard of. Sir H., bewildered, and not knowing whether to think his host a thief or a conjuror, was about to reply, when a servant entered the room, and said his master wished to see him.

Upon this the general clamour against the old man was renewed, and even became louder than before. 'Do not go,' said one; 'Take my advice,' cried another; 'for God's sake do not trust yourself with that old fellow.' The servant protested to Sir H. that he had nothing to fear, and begged that he would follow him to his master. At length he did so, and found his host seated at a table covered with dessert and wine. The gentleman rose on his entrance, and asked pardon for the apparent rudeness he was under the necessity of committing at dinner; 'for,' said he, 'I am Dr Willis, of whom you have probably heard ere this; I confine my practice entirely to cases of insanity, and it is here that I board and lodge my patients. All those with whom you dined are mad, a fact of which I was unwilling to apprize you before, lest it should make you uneasy, and spoil the pleasure of your repast; for though I know them to be perfectly harmless, you very naturally might have entertained apprehensions.'

True Predictions

Sir Robert de Shurland was created a Knight Banneret by Edward I for his valour at the siege of Caerlavoroc Castle. His death has in it something remarkable. Having a quarrel with his priest, he buried the father alive.

The king happened then to lie at anchor under the Isle of Sheepy, and Sir Robert swam on his horse to the royal vessel, obtained his pardon, and swam back to shore on his trusty steed. A witch predicted he would owe his death to that horse; but Sir Robert, who fancied, presumptuously, that he was the arbiter of his own destiny, drew his sword and stabbed his faithful preserver to the heart. Long after, passing the spot, he saw its bones bleaching on the ground: smiling with contempt, he gave the skull a kick; the bone wounded his foot, a mortification ensued, and caused his death.

A fortune-teller once told the celebrated Elizabeth Hardwicke, Countess of Shrewsbury, that she should not die whilst she was building: she accordingly bestowed the greatest part of her immense wealth, which she obtained from her three husbands, in erecting magnificent and spacious seats at Hardwicke, Chatsworth, Bolsover, Oldcotes, and Worksop. The predictions of the Sybil, however, were verified; her ladyship died in a hard frost, when the builders, carpenters, and masons, were disabled from working.

Well-Authenticated Account of Spectres:– From Mr Spink's Journal

'About two o'clock, we saw the island [of Lucera], and all came to an anchor in 12 fathoms of water, and on the 15th of May [1687], we had an observation of Mr Booty in the following manner: Captains Bristo, Brian, and Barnaby shooting of the colues on Strombolo: when we had done we called our men together, about fourteen minutes after three in the afternoon, to our great surprise, we saw two men run by us with amazing swiftness; Captain Barnaby said, "Lord bless me, the foremost man looks like my next-door neighbour, old Booty;" but said he did not know the other behind; Booty was dressed in grey clothes, and the one behind him in black; we saw them run into the burning mountain in the midst of the flames, on which we heard a terrible noise, too horrible to be described; Captain Barnaby then desired us to look at our watches, pen the time down in our pocket books, which we accordingly did.

'When we were laden, we all sailed for England, and arrived at Gravesend on the 6th of October, 1687. Mrs Barnaby and Mrs Brian came to congratulate our safe arrival, and after some discourse, Captain Barnaby's wife says, 'My dead, I have got some news to tell you, old Booty is dead.' He swore an oath, and said we all saw him run into 'hell'. Some time afterwards, Mrs Barnaby met with a lady of her acquaintance in London, and told her what her husband had seen, concerning Mr Booty; it came to Mrs Booty's ears, she arrested Captain Barnaby in £1,000 action, he gave bail, and it came to trial at the court of the King's Bench, where Mr Booty's clothes were brought into the court. The secton of the parish, and the people that were with him when he died, swore to the time when he died, and we swore to our journals, and they came within two minutes; twelve of our men swore that the buttons on his coat were covered with the same grey cloth, and it appeared to be so; the jury asked Mr Spink if he knew Mr Booty in his lifetime, he said he never saw him till he saw him go by him into the burning mountain. The judge then said, "Lord grant I may never see the sight you have seen; one, two, or three, may be mistaken, but twenty or thirty cannot;" so the widow lost the cause.'

Remarkable Superstition

During the season of miracles worked by Bridget of Cheshire, who healed all diseases by prayer, faith, and an embrocation of fasting spittle, multitudes resorted to her from all parts, and kept her salival glands in full employ. Sir John Pryce, with a high spirit of enthusiasm, wrote to this wonderful woman to make him a visit to Newton Hall, in order to restore to him his third and favourite wife. His letter will best tell the foundation on which he built his strange hope, and very uncommon request.

'Madam,– Having received information by various advices, both public and private, that you have of late performed many wonderful cures, even where the best physicians had failed; and the means used appear to be very inadequate to the effects produced; I cannot but look upon you as an extraordinary and high-favoured person. And why may not the same most merciful God, who enables you to restore sight to the blind, hearing to the deaf, and strength to the lame, also enable you to raise the dead to life? Now, having lost a wife, whom I most tenderly loved, my children an excellent step-mother, and our acquaintances a very valuable friend, you will lay us all under the highest obligations: and I earnestly entreat you, for God Almighty's sake, that you will put up your petitions to the throne of grace on our behalf, that the deceased may be restored to us, and the late Dame Eleanor Pryce be raised from the dead. If your personal attendance appear to you to be necessary, I will send my coach and six, and proper servants to wait on you hither, whether you please to appoint. Recompence of any kind, that you could purpose, would be made with the utmost gratitude; but I wish that the bare mention of it be not offensive to both God and you.'

JOHN PRYCE

Superstition Of The Brazilians

Senhor Gama relates a circumstance which occurred during his Ouvidorship, in the Comarca of Sabard, that affords a tolerably strong evidence of the deep subtlety practiced by some, at least, of the Brazilian holy fathers, for their personal benefit. A female residing at no great distance from Sabara, whose mind was darkened by bigotry, and who was particularly rigid in all religious observances, no saint-day passing, without her exhibiting the utmost devotion; mortified herself in a peculiar degree on all occasions of fasting, and during Lent always refrained from eating with such resolution, that she acquired the honour of being considered a saint. So strongly was she influenced by this delusion, that she communicated her self-working inspirations to two or three padres, who lived near. They immediately inflamed her wild imagination by their countenance, and gave public weight to the notion, by affirming that her soul would ascend to heaven on a certain day. Contributions were accordingly talked of for forming an establishment for Santa Harmonica, the name of the female. The priests were, of course, to have the administration of the funds. Good Friday was the appointed day for the consummation of this important event.

The machinery had hitherto worked well, and her exhausted appearance, from continual fasting, warranted the conclusion that her dissolution was near. It was a subject of general interest, and being introduced where the Ouvidor was present, on the evening preceding the intended conclusion of the drama, he stated that he had no faith in any thing so ridiculous; and in the event of the female's death, he would summon an inquest on her body. A friend or coadjutor of the priest was present; he left the party, and hastened on horseback to communicate this determination of the Ouvidor to the holy brethren. An effect, very contrary to the expectations of her devoted worshipers, was thus produced. She speedily recovered from her saintly indisposition, and remains, if not in mental, then at least in bodily health to this day. It was ascertained to have been the intention of the priests, founded on the wicked purpose of deriving advantage from the contemplated establishment of Santa Harmonica, to have produced, by such means, a gradual exhaustion of life by the appointed time.

The Dismal Swamp Of North America

The extensive continent of North America combines most of the various features of the graduations on climate, with numberless objects of admiration to the naturalist peculiar to itself; amongst these may be classed the Dismal Swamp, a morass of an extent unequalled in any part of the known globe. It reaches from Albermarle Sound in North Carolina to the neighbourhood of Portsmouth, on the opposite side of the harbour to Norfolk, and is supposed to contain about 250 square miles, or 150,000 acres.

Some of the interior parts of this vast swampy plain have been seldom explored, the research being full of the utmost perils and dangers; yet some adventurous huntsmen have been found hardy enough to peruse their game within its precincts, although they cannot advance far without great risk of forfeiting their lives to their temerity.

Mr Janson, a late traveller, relates that in one of his excursions, he was often knee-deep; though in other parts the ground supported him firmly. In endeavouring to pass one of these fenny spots, he attempted to avail himself of a bridge formed of the body of a very large tree; when to his great surprise he was immersed in dust to the waist; the tree having become rotten, or probably gutted by insects though it retained its shape and appearance of solidity. Wild beasts lurk in this almost impenetrable recess; cattle also stray there, and often become wild. Hogs are turned into it by their owners to fatten upon the acorns that fall from the oaks. Near the centre of this dreary tract is situated Lake Drummond, or as it is more properly called, the Lake of the Dismal Swamp, which is formed by the drainings of the immense bog. It is crowded with fish of various kinds, which living unmolested, attain a prodigious size. Its surface is generally calm, being sheltered by trees of a lofty size, which grow in abundance on its borders.

The solitude and dangers of this place have given rise to various stories of the most romantic description, that may have been strengthened by the vapours which are continually exhaling from the marshy ground. An anecdote of this kind is currently related by the few inhabitants that dwell near this gloomy tract, and which gave occasion to a beautiful ballad written by Thomas Moore, under the title of 'The Lake of the Dismal Swamp.' A very strong attachment was formed by two natives, who dwelt in that neighbourhood of the swamp. When the death of the female interrupted the felicitous prospect which had opened to their view, this event made such an impression on the mind of the lover, that he lost his senses. His mind became absorbed by her image; and familiar with the scenery of the place, he imagined that she was still alive, and dwelt upon this lake. Determined to find her on whom his soul fixed, he went in pursuit of her; and, as he was never seen afterwards, it is supposed that he perished in some of her dangerous morasses that environ it. The poem may be found in Moore's works, and the images are so appropriate, and the sentiments so pathetic, that the perusal of it will gratify every reader of taste.

No Ghost

The celebrated Marshal Saxe, having arrived with a part of his army at a village where they were to pass the night, purposed sleeping in an apartment in an old castle, which had been long neglected, and was believed to be haunted by spectres, whose nightly yells were often heard by those who dwelt beneath its walls. It was not to be supposed that a warrior like Marshall Saxe was to be terrified, by such reports, from taking possession of his destined chamber. He accordingly went to bed at his usual time; but had not been long asleep, before he was awoke by the most horrid noise his ears had ever heard: and while he was endeavouring to recollect himself, the door of his chamber opened, and a human figure of very large dimensions appeared at the side of his bed. The marshal instantly discharged his pistol at the supposed spectre, which appeared to strike him, as he fell on the floor; he then rose from his bed, and aimed a stroke of his sabre at the figure: but the blade found a resistance, and shivered in his hand. At this moment the apparition rose, and beckoned the general to follow; he obeyed the summons, and attended him to a long gallery, where a trap-door opened, and they sunk into a cavern, which communicated with a subterraneous apartment, occupied by a band of coiners, one of whom, clad in complete armour, traversed the castle every night, to deter every person from inhabiting it. It thus appeared that the steel had resisted the ball, and shivered the marshal's sword; but the villain was knocked down by the force, from which, however, he quickly recovered.

Marshal Saxe, with his usual presence of mind, told them who he was, and laid before them the danger of detaining him, when he had a surrounding army, who would dig to the centre of the earth to find him; but, at the same time, gave them an assurance, that if they would conduct him back to his chamber, he would never relate the history of that night while it could do them harm. The coiners paid a ready obedience to his will, and he kept his word with them, till a subsequent discovery of their retreat gave him full liberty to relate this extraordinary story.

The Terrors Of Death

In 1625, General Walstein, who joined to great intrepidity a large share of enthusiasm, was at Gross Meseritch in Moravia, and completely absorbed in laying the plan of the ensuing campaign. His custom was, to pass part of the night in consulting the stars. One night being at the window lost in consultation, he felt himself violently struck on the back. He turned himself round instantly, knowing that he was alone, and his chamber-door locked; this warrior, bold as he was in battle, was seized with fright. He did not doubt but what this blow was a sign from heaven to warn him of impending danger. He fell into a deep melancholy; nor could any of his friends obtain the secret from him. His confessor, a Capuchin, undertook to discover it, and had art enough to induce one of the pages of the generalissimo to acknowledge, that being intent on playing one of his comrades a trick, he had hid himself in the apartment to which Walstein had retired, and mistaking him for his object, he struck him with all his might. Having discovered his error, while his master was examining the room, he jumped out of the window. The confessor pledged his word of honour to the page, that no evil should befall him, on this account; and he thought himself happy in being able to quiet the trepidations of the general.

But was his despair, when he heard Walstein order the immediate hanging of the rash youth! His orders were absolute; the gibbet was ready; and the page was delivered to the executioner, in the presence of the army. The principal officers of the army were seized with indignation; the lower classes exclaimed against such barbarity; the miserable confessor threw himself repeatedly at the feet of this inexorable commander. The page had mounted the ladder, when suddenly the general cried out, 'Stop!' then with a voice of thunder he said to the page, 'Well, young man, hast thou now experienced what the terrors of death are? I have served you as you served me: now we are quit.'

Spectral Adventure And Superstitious Credulity

Christian, fifth son of Ernest the Pious, obtained certain districts of Altenburg, and fixed his residence at Eisenberg. This prince was a man of an honourable and upright mind, and a tolerable proficient in languages and sciences. In the solitary leisure left him by the concerns of his little state, he fell, however, into the reveries of the alchymists, and fancied that he saw gold and spirits where neither was to be seen. At that time, and for some centuries before, it was a mania common among princes, to strive to increase their wealth and importance by the discovery of the art of making gold; and if they could produce medals of what was termed chemical gold, their happiness was complete.

Christian constructed a complete laboratory, for his favourite pursuit was in correspondence with the most eminent alchymists of his time; and was known to the adepts in England, as well as in Germany, by the name of Theophilus, Abbot of the Blessed Virgin of Lausnitz. The dupe of many a swindler, he at length contracted debts, which he was never able to discharge. He consoled himself with the notion, that spirits would infallibly relieve him from his embarrassments, even when he was necessitated to reduce his establishment, and had but few resources to supply the means of living like a prince. A journal, in the duke's hand-writing, relative to his intercourse with five supposed spirits, and the magnificent promises made by them, is a singular monument of human credulity. It embraces the period between April,

1696, and March, 1706. It appears that the sum promised him by the spirits during this time, if he would have the patience, exceeded five million dollars in ready money, besides bullion and jewels to ten times that amount. The journal contains, moreover, a minute statement of the purposes to which the duke intended to apply these treasures; an estimate of the value of the diamonds and precious stones; and a 'calculation of the prodigious power and energy both of the red and white multiplied and fermented tincture,' reduced with incredible pains and patience into tables; an operation which alone might suffice to turn the brain of an ordinary person.

If the supposed appearances of the spirits which conversed with the duke, and made him such profuse promises, were mere allusions of the imagination, they must have been strange indeed; but the probability is, that they were comedies acted with the deluded alchymist. A Madame von Nnruhe, a confidante of the duke, who is frequently mentioned in his journal, had doubtless performed an important part in these transaction.

Virgilian Predictions Applied To Charles I

Charles I, being at Oxford during the civil wars, went one day to visit the public library. Among the other books he was shewn a very beautiful impression of Virgil. Lord Falkland, who waited on his majesty, thinking to amuse him, proposed consulting the Sortes Virgiliance on his fortune. It is well known our ancestors were much addicted to this sort of superstition. The king smiled, and the first passage that occurred was this: 'That, conquered by a warlike people, driven from his states, separated from his son Ascanius, he should be forced to go and beg foreign succour, that he should see his associates massacred before his eyes; that after making a shameful peace, he should neither enjoy his kingdom nor his life; that he should meet with an untimely death; and that his body should for ever be deprived of a sepulchre.'– The king shewed much uneasiness at this prediction, and Falkland perceiving it, was in a hurry to consult himself the lot in hopes of hitting on some passage that did not relate to his situation, and might divert his majesty's thoughts to other subjects.

Opening the book himself, he found the regrets of Evander for the untimely death of his son:– 'Oh Pallas, thou didst promise not to expose thyself imprudently to the danger of war. It is thus thou hast kept thy promise? Well did I know how much the passion of its glory in its first birth animates a young man, and how far the pleasure of signilizing himself in a first battle may hurry him. Lamentable essay! Fatal actions in the science of arms! Alas! All the gods have been deaf to my solicitations.' Lord Falkland was Secretary of State, was present at the first battle of Newbury, and vigorously charging the rebel cavalry, was killed at the age of thirty-four.

Hardihood Reproved

The strength of imagination has seldom been more forcibly manifested in its influence on a heroic mind, than in the following remarkable instance of its effect upon one who completely denied the possible existence of apparitions, spirits, &c.

In or about the year 1735, the royal vault in King Henry's Chapel, Westminster, was opened for the internment of the body of her majesty. Upon such occasions, it is well known that Westminster Abbey is a place of great resort; many flock thither out of mere curiosity, and others to indulge in their solemn meditation. By the former of these motives, it was that five or six gentlemen, who had dined together at a neighbouring tavern, were induced to visit that famous repository of the titled dead. As they looked down at the steep descent by which so many monarchs had been conveyed to their last resting-place on earth, one exclaimed, 'It is hellish dark;' another stopped his nostrils, and exclaimed against the noisome vapour that ascended from it. Each had his different mode of expression, upon which he saw or felt; but as it is natural for such spectacles to excite some moral reflections, even in most gay and giddy, it will readily be supposed that they all returned with countenances more serious than those with which they entered. Having, however, agreed to pass the evening together, they went back to the same place where they had dined, and the conversation turning upon a future state, apparitions, and spirits, and such topics, one among them, who was a perfect infidel in these matters, especially as to spirits becoming visible, took upon himself to rally the others, who seemed rather inclinable to the contrary opinion.

As it is at all times much easier to deny than it is to prove, especially where those who maintain the negative will not admit as valid any testimonies which can be brought in contradiction to their own opinion – he singly held out against all they had to allege; at length, to end the contest, they proposed to him a wager of twenty guineas, that a great a hero as he pretended, or really imagined himself to be, he had not courage enough to go alone, at midnight, into the vault they had been seeing that day; this he readily accepted, and was very merry at the idea of obtaining such a sum of money with so much ease.

The wager being laid, and the money on both sides deposited in the hands of the landlord of the house, one of the vergers was sent for, who engaged for a piece of gold, to attend the adventurous gentleman to the gate of the cathedral, then shut him in and wait for his return. Matters being thus far arranged, the clock had no sooner struck twelve, than they all set out together; those who had laid the wager, being resolved not to be imposed on by the other's tampering with the verger. As they passed along, however, another scruple arose, which was, that although they might see him enter the church, some convincing proof would be required of his having really gone into the vault; this he instantly removed by pulling his pen-knife from his pocket; 'This,' said he, 'will I stick into the earth, and leave it there for the satisfaction of all parties, and if you do not find it on the inside of the vault, I shall willingly own that I have lost the wager.' This declaration left them nothing to suspect, and friends who were waiting his return at the door of the abbey, were beginning now to believe he had no less resolution than he pretended to. It was now possible that the opinion they had formed was no more than justice; but whatever courage he really had on his first entrance into that ancient and venerable pile, he had no sooner found himself shut into it alone, than (as he afterwards confessed) he felt a kind of shuddering all over him, which he was thoroughly sensible proceeded from something more than the coldness of the night.

Every step he took was echoed by the hollow ground; and though it was not altogether dark, the verger having left a lamp burning just before the door that led to the chapel, without which it would have been impossible for him to have found the place; yet did the faint glimmerings it gave, rather tend to increase than diminish the solemn horrors of every thing around him. He passed on, however, but protested that had not the shame of being laughed at prevented him, he would have forfeited more than twice the sum he had staked, to have been out again. At length after sometimes groping his way, and sometimes directed by the distant lamp, he reached the entrance of the vault; here his inward tremor increased, his limbs shook as if convulsed,– having arrived at the staircase, he stooped forward and stuck his penknife with his whole force in the earth; but, as he was rising to turn back and quit that dreadful place, he felt something, as he thought, suddenly catch hold of him, and pluck him forward; the apprehensions he had previously been in, made an easy way for surprise and terror to seize all his faculties; he lost in an instant every thing that could support him, and fell into a swoon with his head downwards in the vault.

Till one o'clock his friends waited, with some degree of patience for his return, though they thought he staid much longer in that habitation of the silent dead than they imagined a living man would chuse to do; but finding he came not then, they began to apprehend that some accident might have befallen him, as indeed was the case; but as there were many windings and turnings among the tombs, it seemed possible he might have mistaken his way, and be unable to find it again through these recesses. They debated a short time among themselves what they should do in this affair; the verger, they found, though accustomed to the place, did not relish going into the vault alone, at that time of night; accordingly they determined to accompany him, and preceded by a torch, which a footman belonging to one of company had with him, went into the abbey, calling as they went along, as loud as they could, on their king; that wherever he might have wandered to, he could not but hear their voices. No answer, however, being received, they moved on till they came to the stairs of the vault, where looking down, they soon perceived in what posture he lay, and the dismal condition he was in; they immediately ran down to him, rubbed his temples, unbuttoned his clothes, and did every thing they could to recover him, but in vain; and they were obliged to take him up and carry him between them, till they got out of the abbey, when the air coming fresh upon his face, he began to recover himself.

After two or three deep groans – 'Heaven help me! Lord have mercy upon me!' he exclaimed; these words and others of a similar nature, often repeated, very much surprised them; but imagining he was not yet come to his senses, they forbore enquiry till they got him into the tavern, where, having placed him in a chair by the fire-side, they began to ask him how he did, and how he came to be so much disordered; on which he acquainted them with the apprehensions which had seized him immediately after he had left them, and also that, having stuck his penknife into the floor of the vault, according to his agreement, he was about to return with all the speed he could, when something plucked him forward into the vault; but added, that he had neither seen nor heard any thing but what reason might easily account for; and that he should have come back with the same sentiments that he went him, had not the unseen hand convinced him of the injustice of his unbelief.

While he was narrating these occurrences, one of the company perceived the penknife sticking through the fore lappet of his coat, on which presently conjecturing the truth, and finding how deeply his friend was affected (as indeed were all the rest of the company,) not doubting that his return had been impeded by a supernatural hand; he plucked out the pen knife before them all, and cried out, 'Here is the mystery discovered! In the attitude of stooping to stick this knife into the ground, it happened, as you may now plainly perceive, to pass through this coat; and, on your attempting to rise, the terror you were in, magnified this trifling obstruction into an imaginary impossibility of withdrawing yourself, and had an effect on your senses before reason had time to operate.'

This, which it was evident was the case, set every one but the gentleman himself, who had suffered so much by it, laughing immoderately for a while, but it was not easy to draw a smile from him. He ruminated on the affair, while the others were talking gaily about it: and well remembering the agitation he had been in, while he passed through the cathedral, he cried out, 'Well! There is certainly a something after death, or these strange impulses on the mind could never be… I am convinced that I have been too presumptuous; and whether spirits be, or be not permitted to appear, that they exist I ever shall believe.' Firmly fixed in this opinion, he lived and died; nor was it in the power of any of those, who pretended to ridicule this extraordinary change in his sentiments, to bring him back to those which he had formerly entertained.

A Recall From The Grave

Two Parisian merchants, strongly united in friendship, had each one child of different sexes, who early contracted a strong inclination for each other, which was cherished by the parents, and they were flattered by the expectations of being joined for life. Unfortunately, at the time they thought themselves on the point of completing the long wished for union, a man, far advanced in years, and possessed of an immense fortune, cast his eyes on the young lady, and made honourable proposals; her parents could not resist such the temptation of a son-in-law in such affluent circumstances, and forced her to comply. As soon as the knot was tied, she strictly enjoined her former lover never to see her, and patiently submitted to her fate; but the anxiety of her mind preyed on her body, which threw her into a lingering disorder, that apparently carried her off, and she was consigned to the grave.

As soon as this melancholy event reached the lover his affliction was doubled, being deprived of all hopes of her widowhood; but recollecting, that, in her youth she had for some time been in a lethargy, his hopes revived, and hurried him to the place of her burial, where a good bribe procured him the sexton's permission to dig her up, which he performed, and removed her to a place of safety, where, by proper methods, he revived the almost extinguished spark of life. Great was her surprise at finding the state she had been in; and probably as great her pleasure, at the means by which she was recalled from the grave. As soon as she was sufficiently recovered, the lover laid down his claim, and his reasons, supported by a powerful inclination on her side, were too strong for her to resist: but as France was no longer a place of safety for them, they agreed to remove to England, where they continued ten years, when a strong inclination of revisiting their native country seized them, which they thought they might safely gratify, and accordingly performed their voyage.

The lady was so unfortunate as to be known by her old husband, whom she met in a public walk, and all her endeavours to disguise herself were ineffectual: he laid his claim to her before a court of justice, and the lover defended his right, alleging, the husband, by burying her, had forfeited his title, and that he had acquired a just one, by freeing her from the grave, and delivering her from the jaws of death. These reasons, however, whatever weight they might have had with the court where love presided, seemed to have little effect on the grave sages of the law: and the lady, with her lover, not thinking it safe to wait the determination of the court, prudently retired a second time out of the kingdom.

Effects Of Fortune Telling

A few years since, a young lady, whose name and address must, for very obvious reasons, be concealed, when in the full possession of her health and spirits, forewarned by a gipsey, by whom she, in a mere frolic, had the curiosity to have her fortune told, that she would assuredly die on a certain day, within a few months from that time. This wanton and idle prediction gradually made a strong and unusual impression on the girl's mind. Her dejection and alteration of manner being observed by her friends, she was asked the cause, upon which she related the cause just mentioned, adding, that she felt conscious the prediction would be verified. Her friends, of course, at first endeavoured to laugh her out of the idea; but when they perceived, notwithstanding, her melancholy daily increase, they had recourse to reasoning and remonstrance on the absurdity of indulging in such a mere air-drawn phantom. Ridicule and remonstrance proved equally ineffectual. The poor girl at length becoming seriously ill, took to her bed, from which she never more arose. As the time of the prophecy grew nearer, she grew visibly worse, and on the very day foretold by the gipsey, she expired, under all the fictitious horrors of a deluded imagination.

A Military Necromancer

When Marshal Lannes served with Bonaparte in the grand campaigns of Italy, nearly all the generals of that fortunate army were young. They accordingly often met to amuse

114

themselves; and the joy which success inspired added to the gaiety of youth. One day while they were assembled at Bonaparte's quarters, the conversation turned on oracles, although there was by no means much credulity amongst the party. Bonaparte, in order to entertain the company, announced his intention of telling all their fortunes. The military necromancer took their hands alternately, examined the lineaments, and seemed to utter any extravagance that struck his fancy. Bursts of laughter of course followed every prediction.

It came to the turn of Lannes; Bonaparte took his hand, looked at it, dropped it without saying a word, and passed to another. Lannes asked the reason of this silence. To avoid replying, the general-in-chief discontinued the amusement, as if he thought the child's play had lasted long enough. Lannes insisted. 'Let us be done with it,' said Bonaparte, 'you see it is only a bit of folly.' The curiosity of Lannes was, however, too strongly excited; he returned to the charge, and at last Bonaparte yielded, and took his hand. 'Do you see that line?' said he, 'it prognosticates that you are to be killed by a cannon-ball.' 'Indeed,' replied he, laughing, 'if it does not come soon, there will be no place for it to hit.' He had then fifteen wounds on his body, and had received thirty-two, when he was killed by a cannon-ball at the battle of Wagram.

It may be observed, by the by, that this pleasantry of Bonaparte, so unfortunately verified, was not likely to compromise his prophetic character. He might, with perfect safety, predict the killing of his generals by cannon-balls. Some of his prophecies must necessarily have proved true; and one prediction fulfilled is quite sufficient to make the fortune of a sorcerer.

Driving Out The Devil

Among the various complaints which in Abyssinia are said
to be caused by the devil, there is one of a very curious
description, called the Tegretier, and of which the following account is given by Pearse, an English sailor, who had
resided in that country many years.

'A complaint, called the tegretier, both in Tegri and
Ammerrer, which is not so frequent among men as women,
is for a certainty very surprising; and I think the devil must
have some hand in it. It is very common among them; and
when I have been told in what manner they acted, I would
never believe it until it came to my own wife's chance,
who had lived with me five years. At the first appearance
of this complaint, she was five or six days very ill, and her
speech so much altered, that I could scarcely understand
her. Her friends and relations came to visit her, told me her
complaint was the tegretier, which, from what I had heard,
frightened me, and I would at the instant have turned her
away, only for fear they might think me a brute for turning
away my wife when afflicted by sickness. Her parents, however, persuaded me to bear it with patience, and say nothing,
for if I were to be angry it would cause her death, and they
would cure her as all others were cured in this country.

After the first five or six days' sickness, she began to be
continually hungry, and would eat five or six times in the
night, never slept, and in the day time she would go about,
followed by some one of her parents, to all her neighbours,

borrowing rings and other ornaments for the neck, arms, and legs. I did not like the thing at all; but for the sake of seeing the curiosity, I endeavoured to hold my tongue and be patient. Her speech I could scarcely understand; and she, like all others troubled with this complaint, called a man she, and a woman he. One day she called unto me in the presence of her friends after the manner of calling a woman, which vexed me so much, that I said she should not stop in the house. But the moment she saw me in a passion, she fell as if in a fit, and I can assure you that I saw the blood run from her eyes as if they had been pricked with a lance.'

Pearce, though not a very doting husband, did not wish to lose his wife, when means could be used to save her; he therefore determined to say nothing more until the day appointed for her cure, or 'the devil to be drove out of her;' which was done in the following manner:–

'Her friends had hired as many trumpeters and drum-mers who go about the country for the purpose, as they thought sufficient; and early in the morning of the day appointed, they loaded her neck, arms, and legs, with silver ornaments, and dressed her with a dress which the great men wear at reviews after battle, which the owners readily lent on such an occasion. After she was sufficiently dressed, she was taken to a plain appointed by herself, about a mile from the town, where hundreds of boys, girls, and men and women of low class, follow. Her friends and relations take a great many large jars of *maize* and *swoir* for them to drink; I had often seen people go out of town for the same purpose, but would not for shame follow to see them. However, for the sake of curiosity, I was determined to see the last of this, and I therefore went to the place appointed before day-light, and waited until they came; a cradle was placed in the middle of the spot, covered with a large carpet, and a great many large jars of maize were placed round it. As soon as she came near, she began to dance, and the trumpeters all began to play in two parties; when one party was tired, the other relieved them, so that the noise might constantly be heard; the drink being continually served out by her friends to all, kept them singing and shouting; she still dancing and jumping, sometimes four or five feet from the ground, and every now and then she would take off an ornament and throw it down. Some one being appointed to take care that they might not be lost, picked them up, and put them in a basket. She kept on jumping and dancing in this manner without the least appearance of being tired, until nearly sun-set, when she dropped the last ornament, and as soon as the sun disappeared, she started; and I am perfectly sure, that for as good as four hundred yards, when she dropped as if dead, the fastest running man in the world could not have come up with her.

The fastest running young man that can be found, is employed by her friends to run after her with a matchlock well loaded, so as to make a good report; at the moment she starts, he starts with her, but before she has run the distance where she drops as if dead, he is left half way behind; as soon as he comes up to her, he fires right over her body, and asks her name, which she then pronounces, although, during the time of her complaint, she denies her Christian name, and detests all priests or churches. Her friends afterwards take her to church, where she is washed with holy water, and is thus cured.' Thus ends the ceremony of 'Driving out the Devil.'

The Trance Of Mrs Godfrey

This lady had been a long time ill in consequence of the recent death of her brother, but one Sunday, fancying herself better than she had been for some time, able to go to chapel, as she was dressing for the purpose, she suddenly fell down to all appearance dead. The screams of her women brought Colonel Godfrey into the room, who directed that his lady should immediately be put to bed, and that two persons should constantly continue with her, till indubitable symptoms appeared of her decease, notwithstanding the opinions of the physicians, that the breath of life was irrevocably departed; and in opposition to the solicitations of his friends to have the body interred, he continued determined in his resolution to the contrary till the Sunday following; when exactly at the same hour on which the change had happened, signs appeared of returning sensibility. So punctual was the nature in her operations upon this singular occasion, that Mrs Godfrey awoke from her trance just as the chapel bell was once more ringing; which so perfectly eradicated from her memory every trace of insensibility, that she blamed her attendants for not awaking her in time to go to church, as she had proposed to do. Colonel Godfrey, whose tenderness for his lady was unremitted, gave orders that she should by no means be made acquainted with what happened, so that she remained ignorant of the transaction to the day of her death.

Story of Macpherson

It was about the year 1805, that Major Macpherson and a few gentlemen of his acquaintance, with their attendants, went out to hunt in the middle of the tremendous range of mountains which rise between Athol and Badenoch. Many are the scenes are of wild grandeur and rugged deformity which amaze the wanderer in the Grampian deserts; but none of them surpass this in wildness and still solemnity.

In the afternoon they stepped into a little bothy or resting place that stood by the side of a rough mountain stream, and having meat and drink, they abandoned themselves to mirth and jollity.

This Major Macpherson was said to have been guilty of some acts of extreme cruelty and injustice in raising recruits in that country, and was on that account held in detestation by the common people. He was otherwise a respectable character and of honourable connexions, as were the gentlemen who accompanied him.

When their hilarity was at the highest pitch, ere ever they were aware, a young man stood before them, of a sedate, mysterious appearance, looking sternly at the Major. Their laughter was hushed in a moment, for they had not observed any human being in the glen, save those of their own party, nor did they so as much as perceive when their guest entered. Macpherson appeared particularly struck, and somewhat shocked at the sight of him; the stranger beckoned to the Major, who followed him instantly out of the bothy. The curiosity of the party was aroused, and they watched their motions with great punctuality; they walked a short way down the side of the river, and appeared in earnest conversation for a few minutes, and from some involuntary motions of their bodies, the stranger seemed to be threatening Macpherson, and the latter interceding; they parted, and though not above twenty yards distant, before the Major got half way back to the bothy, the stranger was gone, and they saw no more of him.

But what was extraordinary, after the dreadful catastrophe, though the most strict and extended inquiry was made, neither the stranger, nor his business could be discovered. The countenance of the Major was so visibly altered on his return, and bore such evident marks of trepidation, that the mirth of the party was marred during the remainder of the excursion, and none of them cared to ask him any questions concerning his visitant, or the errand he came on.

This was early in the week; and on the Friday immediately following, Macpherson proposed to his companions a second expedition to the mountains. They all objected on account of the weather, which was broken and rough; but he persisted in his resolution, and finally told them that he must and would go, and those who did not choose to accompany him might tarry at home. The consequence was, that the same party, with the exception of one man, went again to hunt in the forest of Glenmore.

Although none of them returned the first night after their departure, that was little regarded, it being customary for the sportsmen to lodge occasionally in the bothies of the forest; but when Saturday night arrived, and no word from them, their friends became greatly alarmed. On Sunday, servants were dispatched to all the inns and gentlemen's houses in the bounds, but no accounts of them could be learned. One solitary dog only returned, and he was wounded and maimed. The alarm spread: a number of people, and in the utmost consternation, went to search for friends among the mountains. When they reached the fatal bothy (dreadful to relate!) they found the dead bodies of the whole party lying scattered about the place. Some of them were considerably mangled, and one nearly severed in two. Others were not marked by any wounds, of which number I think it was said the Major was one, who was lying flat on his face. It was a scene of woe, lamentation, and awful astonishment, none being able to account for what had happened: but it was visible it had not been effected by any human agency. The bothy was torn from its foundations, and scarcely a vestige of it was left; its very stones were all scattered about in different directions; there was one huge corner-stone in particular, which twelve men could scarcely have raised, that was tossed to a considerable distance, yet no marks of fire or water were visible.

Extraordinary as this story may appear, and an extraordinary story it certainly is, I have not the slightest cause to doubt the certainty of the leading circumstances; with regard to the rest, you had them as I had them. In every mountainous district in Scotland, to this day, a belief in supernatural agency prevails, in a greater or lesser degree. Such an awful dispensation as the above, was likely to rekindle every lingering spark in it.

Barbarity Of the Native Tribes Of Missouri

The power of some of the former rulers of the Osmahaws is said to be almost absolute. That of the celebrated Black Bird (Wash-ing-guh-sah-ba,) seems to have been actually so, and was retained undimished until his death, which occurred in the year 1800, of the small pox, which then almost desolated his nation. Agreeably to these orders, he was interred in a sitting posture on his favourite horse, upon the summit of a high bluff of the Missouri, 'that he might see the white people ascending the river to trade with his nation.' A mound was raised over his remains, on which food was regularly placed for many years afterwards: but this rite has been discontinued, and the staff, that on its summit supported a white flag, has no longer existence.

The chief appears to have possessed extraordinary mental abilities, but he resorted to the most nefarious means to establish firmly the supremacy of his power. He gained the reputation of the greatest of medicine men; and his medicine, which was no other than arsenic itself, that had been furnished him for the purpose, by the villany of the traders, was secretly administered to his enemies or rivals. Those persons who offended him, or counteracted his views, were removed agreeably to his prediction, and all opposition silenced, apparently by the operation of his potent spells. Many were the victims to his unprincipled ambition, and the nation stood in awe of him as of the supreme arbiter of his fate. He delighted in the display of his power, and, on one occasion, during a national hunt, accompanied by the white man, they arrived on the bank of a fine flowing stream, and although all were parched with thirst, no one but the white man was permitted to taste of the water. As the chief thought proper to give no reason for this severe punishment, it seemed to be the result of caprice.

One inferior, but distinguished chief, called the Little Bow, at length opposed his power. This man was a warrior of high renown, and so popular in the nation, that it was remarked of him, that he enjoyed the confidence and best wishes of the people, while his rival reigned in terror. Such an opponent could not be brooked, and the Black Bird endeavoured to destroy him. On one occasion the Little Bow returned to the lodge, after the absence of a few days on an excursion. His wife placed before him his accustomed food; but the wariness of the Indian character led him to observe some peculiarity in her behaviour, which assured him that all was not right; he questioned her concerning the food she had set before him, and the appearance of her countenance, and her replies so much increased his suspicions, that he compelled her to eat the contents of the bowl. She then confessed that the Black Bird had induced her to mingle with the food a portion of his terrible medicine, in order to destroy him. She fell a victim to the machinations of the Black Bird, who was thus disappointed of his object.

With a band of nearly two hundred followers, the Little Bow finally seceded from the nation, and established a separate village on the Missouri, where they remained until the death of the tyrant.

On one occasion, the Black Bird seems to have been touched with remorse, or perhaps by penitence, in his career of enormity. One of his squaws having been guilty of some trifling offence, he drew his knife, in a paroxysm of rage, and stabbed her to the heart. After viewing the dead body a few moments, he seated himself near it, and covering himself with his robe, he remained immovable for three days, without taking any nourishment. His people vainly petitioned that he would 'have pity on them', and unveil his face; he was deaf to all remonstrances, and the opinion prevailed that he intended to die of starvation. A little child was at length brought in by its parent, who gently raised the leg of the chief, and placed the neck of the child beneath his foot. The murderer then rose, harangued his people, and betook himself to his ordinary occupations.

Towards the latter part of his life, he became very corpulent, the consequent of indolence and repletion. He was transported by carriers, on a bison robe, to the various feasts to which he was daily invited; and should the messenger find him asleep, they dared not awaken him by a noise or by shaking, but by respectfully tickling his nose with a straw.

Terrific Spectral Appearance

Professor Koempfer, of the University of Strasburgh, in the former part of his life, resided at Frankfort on the Maine, where he exercised the profession of physician. One day being invited to dine with a party of gentlemen, after dinner, an animated conversation commenced, and at length the discourse turned upon apparitions &c. Koempfer was amongst those who strenuously combatted the idea of supernatural visitations, as preposterous and absurd in the highest degree. A gentleman, who was a captain in the army, with equal zeal supported the opposite side of the question.

The question was long and warmly contended, both being men of superior talents, till in the end the attention of the whole company was engrossed by the dispute. At length the captain proposed to Koempfer to accompany him that evening to his country house, where, if he did not convince him of supernatural agency, he would then allow himself in the estimation of present company, to whom he appealed as judges of the controversy, to be defeated. The professor with a laugh instantly consented to the proposal, if the captain, on his honour, would promise that no trick should be played off upon him; the captain readily gave his word and honour that no imposition should be resorted to.

The company broke up at rather an early hour, and the Captain and Keompfer set out together on their spiritual adventure. When they drew near the Captain's house, he suddenly stopped near the entrance to a solemn grove of trees. They descended from their vehicle, and walked towards the grove. The Captain traced a large circle in the ground, into which he requested Koempfer to enter. He then solemnly asked him if he possessed sufficient resolution to remain there alone to complete the adventure; to which Koempfer replied in the affirmative. He added further, 'whatsoever you may witness stir not, I charge you, from this spot, till you see me again; if you step beyond this circle, it will be your immediate destruction.' He then left the professor to his own meditations, who could not refrain from smiling at what he thought in the assumed solemnity of the acquaintance, and the whimsical situation in which he was placed.

The night was clear and frosty, and the stars shone with a peculiar brilliancy: he looked around on all sides to observe from whence he might expect his ghostly visitant. He directed his regards towards the grove of trees; he perceived a small spark of fire at a considerable distance. It advanced nearer; he then concluded it was a torch borne by some person who was in the Captain's secret, and who was to personate a ghost. It advanced nearer and nearer – the light increased – it approached the edge of the circle wherein he was placed. 'It was then,' to use his own expressions, 'I seemed surrounded with a fiery atmosphere; the heavens and every object before visible was excluded from my sight.' But now a figure of the most indefinable description absorbed his whole attention; his imagination had never yet conceived any thing so truly fearful. What appeared to him the more remarkable, was an awful benignity portrayed in his countenance, and with which it seemed to regard him. He contemplated for a while this dreadful object, but at length fear began insensibly to arrest his faculties. He sunk down on his knees to implore the protection of heaven; he remarked, for his eyes were still riveted on the mysterious appearance, which remained stationary, and earnestly regarded him, that at every repetition of the name of the Almighty, it assumed a more benignant expression of countenance, whilst a terrific brilliancy gleamed from its eyes. He fell prostrate on the ground, imploring heaven to remove him from the object of his terrors. After a while he raised his head, and beheld the mysterious light fading by degrees in the gloomy shades of the grove from which it issued.

It soon entirely disappeared, and the Captain joined him almost at the same moment. During their walk to the Captain's house, which was close at hand, the Captain asked his companion, 'Are you convinced that what you have now witnessed was supernatural?' Koempfer replied, 'he could not give a determinate answer to the question; he could not on natural principles account for what he had seen, it certainly was not like any thing earthly, he therefore begged to be excused from saying any more on a subject he could not comprehend.' The Captain replied, 'he was sorry he was not convinced,' and added with a sigh, 'he was still more sorry that he had ever tried to convince him.'

Thus far it may be considered no more than a common phantasmagorical trick, played off on the credulity of the Professor, but in the end the performer payed dearly for his exhibition: he had, like a person ignorant of a complicated piece of machinery, given impetus to a power which he had not the knowledge to control, and which in the end proves fatal to him who puts it in motion. Immediately after supper the Captain ordered all his servants to bed. It drew towards midnight, and he remained still absorbed in thought, but apparently not wishing to retire to bed. Koempfer was silently sitting smoking his pipe, when, on a sudden, a heavy step was heard in the passage; it approached the room in which they were sitting – a knock was heard: the Captain raised his head and looked mournfully at Koempfer. The knock was repeated – both were silent: a third knock was heard, and Koempfer broke the silence by asking his friend why he did not order the person in. Ere the Captain could reply, the room door was flung wildly open, when behold! the same dreadful appearance which Koempfer had already witnessed stood in the door-way. Its awful benignity of countenance was now changed into the most appalling and terrific frown. A large dog which was in the room crept whining and trembling behind the Captain's chair. For a few moments the figure remained stationary, and then motioned the Captain to follow it: he rushed towards the door – the figure receded before him, and Koempfer determined to accompany his friend, followed with the dog.

They proceeded unobstructed into the court-yard; the doors and gates seemed to open spontaneously before them. From the court-yard they passed into the open fields; Koempfer, with the dog, were about twenty or thirty paces behind the Captain. At length they reached the spot near the entrance to the grove, where the circle was traced; the figure stood still, when on a sudden a bright column of flame shot up, a loud shriek was heard, a heavy body seemed to fall from a considerable height, and in a moment all was silence and darkness. Koempfer called loudly on the

Captain, but received no answer. Alarmed for the safety of his friend, he fled back to the house, and quickly assembled the family. They proceeded to the spot, and found the apparently lifeless body of the Captain stretched on the ground. The professor ascertained, on examination, that the heart still beat faintly; he was instantly conveyed home, and all proper means were resorted to to restore animation; he revived a little, and seemed sensible of their attentions, but remained speechless till his death, which took place three days after. Down one side, from head to foot, the flesh was livid and black, as if from a fall or severe bruise. The affair was hushed up so the immediate neighbourhood, and his sudden death was attributed to apoplexy.

Extraordinary Case Of Apparent Death

A young lady, an attendant of the princess of Zell, after having been confined to her bed for a great length of time, with a violent nervous disorder, was at last, to all appearance, deprived of life. Her lips were quite pale, her face resembled the countenance of a dead person, and her body grew cold. She was removed from the room in which she died, was laid in a coffin, and the day of her funeral was fixed on. The day arrived, and her body grew cold. She was removed from the room in which she died, and, according to the custom of the country, funeral songs and hymns were sung before the door. Just as the people were about to nail on the lid of the coffin, a kind of perspiration was observed on the surface of her body, and she shortly after recovered. The following is the account she gave of her sensations: she said, 'It seemed to her as if in a dream, that she was really dead; yet she was perfectly conscious of all that happened around her. She distinctly heard her friends speaking and lamenting her death at the side of her coffin. She felt them pull on the dead clothes, and lay her in it. This feeling produced a mental anxiety she could not describe. She tried to cry out, but her mind was without power, and could not act on her body. She had the contradictory feeling as if she were in her own body and not in it at the same time. It was equally impossible for her to stretch out her arm, to open her eyes to cry, although she continually endeavoured to do so. The internal anguish of her mind was at its utmost height, when the funeral hymns began to be sung, and when the lid of the coffin was about to be nailed on. The thought that she was to be buried alive was the first which gave activity to her mind, and enabled it to operate on her corporeal frame.'

Interesting Narrative Of A Journey To The African Kingdom Of Dahomey

In passing by the market-place of Grigwhee, I found a great number of people collected there; and observing some large umbrellas among them, I concluded that the viceroy and his caboceers were of the party. Surprised at this early assembly, I sent a servant to inquire the cause of it: but before he could return, a messenger from the viceroy, who had discovered my approach, accosted me from his master, requesting to speak with me before my departure. I found

him passing sentence of death on a criminal, a middle-aged woman who was on her knees before him, in the midst of a circle formed by his attendants. I requested for her life to be spared; and, from the very circumstance of having sent for me, flattered myself that my offer of purchasing her for a slave would be accepted; but I was disappointed. He told me the king himself had considered the offence and decreed the sentence; which was, 'that her head should be cut off, and fixed on a stake,' that was lying by her, and which she had been compelled to bring with her from Abomey for that purpose.

During this conversation a little girl prompted by curiosity, made her way through the crowd; and discovering her mother, ran to her with joy to congratulate her on her return. The poor woman, after a short embrace, said,

'Go away my child, this is no place for you,' and she was immediately conveyed away. The viceroy proceeded in his sentence, which the poor wretch heard with seeming indifference, picking her teeth with a straw, which she had taken from the ground. When the viceroy concluded his charge to the spectators, of obedience, submission, and orderly behaviour, which the king required from all his people, the delinquent received a blow on the back of her head with a bludgeon, from one of the executioners, which levelled her to the ground; when another, with a cutlass, severed it from her body. The head was then fixed on a pole, in the market-place, and the body immediately carried to the outside of the town, and left there to be devoured by the wild beasts.

The person executed, had kept one of the little shops in the market, having discovered, a few days before, that some trifle had been stolen from her, had taken from the fire a lighted stick, which whilst she waved round her head (a usual custom in that country), she expressed a wish that the person who had taken her property, and did not restore it, might die, and be extinguished like that stick. In going through the ceremony, a spark had fallen on the thatch of one of the huts, and set the market on fire.

I had occasion to visit Abomey again in December, 1773. The king was then infirm, and sinking under years as well as disease; he was confined to his chamber, but, desiring to see me, gave me an opportunity of inspecting his private apartment. It was a neat detached room for sleeping in, separated from the court in which it stood, by a wall about breast-high, the top of which was stuck full of human lower jaw-bones. The little area within it was paved with skulls; which I understood were those of neighbouring kings, and other persons of eminence and distinction, whom, having been taken prisoners in the course of his wars, he had placed them there, that he might literally enjoy the savage gratification of trampling on the heads of his enemies. He did not long survive this interview, but lingered on till the 17th of May, 1774, when he died, aged near seventy years, of which he had reigned about forty, and was succeeded by his son Adahunzu.

Vision Of Charles XI Of Sweden

The following singular narrative occurs in the Rev. J. T. James's Travels in Sweden, Prussia, Poland, &c, during the years 1813 and 1814.— The most marvellous part of the affair is, that, no less than six persons (the monarch inclusive) concur in attesting the reality of the pretended vision.

Charles XI, it seems, sitting in his chamber between the hours of eleven and twelve at night, was surprised at the appearance of a light in the window of the hall of the diet: he demanded of the grand chancellor, Bjelke, who was present, what he saw, and was answered that it was only the reflection of the moon; with this, however, he was dissatisfied; and a senator soon after entering the room, he addressed the same question to him, but received the same answer. Looking afterwards again through the window, he thought he observed a crowd of persons in the hall. Ordering the two noblemen above-mentioned, as also Oxenstiern and Brabe, to accompany him, he sent for Grunsten the door-keeper, and descended the staircase leading to the hall.

Here the party seemed so sensible of a certain degree of trepidation, and no one else daring to open the door, the king took the key, unlocked it, and entered first into the anti-chamber: and to their infinite surprise, it was fitted up with black cloth: alarmed at his extraordinary circumstance, a second pause occurred; at length the king set his foot within the hall, but fell back with astonishment at what he saw; again, however, taking courage, he made his companions promise to follow him, and advanced. The hall was lighted up and arrayed with the same mournful hanging as the anti-chamber: in the centre was a round table, where sat sixteen venerable men, each with large volumes lying open before them: above was the king, a young man of sixteen or eighteen years of age, with the crown on his head and sceptre in his hand. On his right hand sat a personage about forty years of age, whose face bore the strongest marks of integrity; on the left an old man of seventy, who seemed very urgent with the young king that he should make a certain sign with his head, which as often as he did, the venerable men struck their hands on their books with violence.

'Turning my eyes,' said the king, 'a little further, I beheld a scaffold and executioners, and men with their clothes tucked up, cutting off heads one after the other so fast, that the blood formed a deluge on the floor: those who suffered were all young men. Again I looked up, and perceived the throne behind the great table almost overturned; near to it stood a man of forty, who seemed the protector of the kingdom. I trembled at the sight of these things, and cried aloud – 'It is the voice of God! – What ought I to understand? When shall all this come to pass?' A dead silence prevailed, but on crying out a second time, the young king answered me, saying, 'This shall not happen in your time, but in the days of the sixth sovereign after you. He shall be of the same age as I appear to be, and this personage sitting besides me, gives you the air of him that shall be regent and protector of the realm. During the last year of the regency, the country shall be sold by certain young men, but he shall then take up the cause, and, acting in conjuction with the young king, shall establish the throne on a sure footing; and this is such a way, that never was before, or ever afterwards shall be seen in Sweden so great a king. All the Swedes shall be happy under him; the public debts shall be paid; he shall leave many millions in the treasury, and shall not die but at a very advanced age; yet before he is firmly seated on the throne, there shall be an effusion of blood take place unparalleled in history. You,' added he, 'who are king of this nation, see that he is advertised of these matters: you have seen all: act according to your wisdom.'

Having said this, the whole vanished, and (adds he) we saw nothing but ourselves and our flambeaus, while the anti-chamber through which we passed, on returning was no longer clothed in black.

Gross Credulity and Ignorance

Sir John Reresby, in his memoirs, gives a strong instance that good sense is not always incompatible with an attach-ment to the most gross absurdities which can be gleaned from the nursery.

After he has spoken of a witch, whose person, he, as gov-ernor of York, had the custody of, he modestly hints that he was not fully persuaded of her guilt, although the court had condemned her, but at the same time thinks it right to tell a story, which appears to have staggered him, and which he recites upon the credit of a sentinel, who was on duty before the door of said witch's dungeon. 'One of my soldiers,' says Sir John, 'being upon guard, about eight o'clock at night, at the gate of Clifford Tower the very night after the witch was arraigned, he heard a great noise at the castle; and, going to the porch, he there saw a scroll of paper creep from under the door, which, as he imagined, by moonshine, turned first into a monkey, and thence assumed the form of a turkey-cock, which passed to and fro by him. Surprised at this, he went to the prison, where the witch was confined, and called the under-keeper, who came and saw the scroll dance up and down, and creep under the door, where there was an opening of the thickness of a half crown.'

Here Sir John Reresby breaks off his narrative, leaving this extraordinary story, as he justly calls it, and which, he says, he had from the two parties who were present, 'to be believed or to be disbelieved, as the reader shall be inclined this way or that.'

Haunted Bed Room

Professor Gassendi, in one of his letters, says, that he was consulted by his friend and patron, the Count D'Alais, governor of Provence, on phenomenon that haunted his bed-chamber, while he was at Marseilles, on some business relative to his office.

The count told Gassendi that for several successive nights, as soon as the candle was taken away, he and his countess saw a luminous spectre, sometimes of an oval, and sometimes of a triangular form; that it always immediately disappeared when a light was brought into the room; that he often struck at it, but could discover nothing solid. Gassendi, as a natural philosopher, endeavoured to account for it; sometimes attributing it to some defect of vision, or to some dampness of the apartment; insinuating, that perhaps it might be sent from heaven to him, to give him warning in due time of something that would happen. The spectre still continued its visits all the time that he stayed at Marseilles.

Some years afterwards, on their return to Aix, the countess D'Alais confessed to her husband that she played him this trick, by means of one of her women placed under her bed with a phial of phosphorus, with an intention to frighten him away from Marseilles, a place in which she disliked to live.

Extraordinary Delusion:–
From Madame Du Noyer's Letters

'The following story will appear to you incredible and fabulous, and perhaps I need not assure you I had great difficulty in believing it; but as I had it from the lips of the individual who forms the subject of it, and as he was visionary, I attributed it to the effects of a disturbed imagination. The event (as least as far as this person's mind was concerned) occurred in our day, and is attested by many in the city of

Nismes. The tale is told thus: Mr Graverol was alone in his study one day, about two o'clock in the afternoon when a stranger was ushered in. As soon as he was seated, a conversation started up between the two. The stranger addressed Mr G. in elegant Latin, saying, that he had heard his learning spoken highly of, and he had come from a distant country to converse with him on things which had embarrassed the ancient philosophers. After Mr G. had replied suitably to the compliment offered to his talents, some very abstruse subject was introduced, and handled in a scientific manner. The stranger did not confine himself to the Latin language, but he spoke some Greek and some Eastern tongues, which Mr G. also understood perfectly. The latter was astonished and delighted with his guest's profound information; and for fear some person should call on him and interrupt the conversation, he proposed a walk, which was readily acceded to by the stranger.

'The day was delightful, and you know there are some beautiful walks in the neighbourhood of Nismes. They left the house with the design of going through the gate called the Crown-gate, which leads to some gardens and a very fine avenue of noble trees: but as Mr Faverol's house was a considerable distance from the place mentioned, they were obliged to cross several streets before they reached it. During the walk, Mr G. was observed by many of his acquaintances, he being well-known in the city, to use much gesture, and he was also noticed speaking at intervals: what added to the surprise was, that no person was seen accompanying him. Some of his friends sent to his wife, expressing their fears that he was deranged, describing the manner in which he was noticed to pass through the streets. She, being greatly alarmed at intelligence so extraordinary, despatched several persons in search of him; but they could not find him, as he had gained the shady walks outside the city with his new acquaintance.

After expiating on the subjects of ancient and modern philosophy, and reasoning on the secrets of nature, they entered on the wide fields of magic and enchantment. The stranger argued with great ingenuity and power, but he exceeded the bounds of probability; and Mr G. cried out, 'Stop, stop! Christianity forbids us proceeding to such lengths – we should not pass the prescribed boundaries.' He had no sooner said this (at least according to the narration spread abroad) than the stranger vanished. Mr Graverol being at that moment at the extreme end of one of the avenues, which was terminated by some palisades, was compelled to return the same way he went. On turning round, and not perceiving his companion, he became greatly alarmed, and uttered a dreadful shriek, which brought some men, who were employed pruning the trees, to him. When these people perceived how pale and frightened he was, they gave him some wine which they had in a flagon, and used all the means they could devise to restore him to himself.

'As soon as he recovered his recollection, he inquired if they had noticed where the gentleman had gone with whom he had been walking. He was very much agitated when these good people informed him that no one was with him when he passed under the trees where they were at work; neither had a single individual been in his company since he came into their sight, and they had observed him some distance before he reached them. They added, moreover, that when he passed, it struck them as being somewhat singular that he should be so deeply engaged in apparent conversation, although he was alone.

Mr Graverol, on learning this, went immediately home, where he found his house in disorder and alarm concerning the reports which had reached his wife. He then related his adventure. When the story was noised abroad, it was publicly asserted all over the city that the devil had visited Mr Graverol. He was a very gentlemanlike man and an advocate, and related the circumstances to me as I have detailed them. When he concluded, he said, 'This is accurately what happened: you are now acquainted with the facts as well as myself, and you may exercise your judgement respecting them as shall best seem fit. And all that I can add is, the stranger was a very learned and eloquent man, and reasoned like a philosopher.'

And finally....

Resuscitation

In the year 1728, Margaret Dickson was tried at Edinburgh for the murder of her child, supposed to have been born during the absence of her husband. After her condemnation, she behaved in the most penitent manner, acknowledged her infidelity, but constantly and steadily denied that she had murdered her child, or even formed an idea of so horrible a crime. At the place of execution, her behaviour was consistent with her former declaration, and she was hanged. After her execution, her body was cut down, and delivered to her friends, who put it into a cart, to be buried at her native place; but the weather being sultry, the

persons who had the body in charge, stopped to drink at a village about two miles from Edinburgh. While they were refreshing themselves, one of them perceived the lid of the coffin move, and uncovering it, the woman immediately sat up, when most of the spectators ran off with every sign of trepidation. A person who was drinking in the house, had recollection enough to bleed her; in about an hour she was put to bed, and next morning she so far recovered, as to be able to walk to her own house. By the Scottish law, which is partly founded on that of the Romans, a person against whom the judgement of the court has been executed, can suffer no more in future, but is thenceforth totally exculpated; and it is likewise held, that the marriage is dissolved by the execution of the convicted party. Mrs Dickson having been thus convicted and executed, the king's advocate could prosecute her no farther, but he filed a bill in the High Court of Justiciary, against the Sheriff, for omitting to fulfil the law. The husband of this restored convict, married her publicly in a few days after she was hanged; and she lived about thirty years afterwards.

Tales from the Terrific Register
The Book of Wonders

EDITED BY CATE LUDLOW
978 07524 5265 4

This selection contains the most startling tales from this 185-year-old publication. Amongst the prodigious marvels contained herein you will find giants, children with horns and babies brought up by wolves, uncanny dreams, devils, and attacks by cannibals, snakes, rats, crocodiles, and bears. Other wonders include 'the ferocious attack of a lioness on the Exeter mail', and a man bitten twenty times by a shark whilst fishing in Yorkshire.

Tales from the Terrific Register
The Book of Murder

EDITED BY CATE LUDLOW
978 07524 5266 1

Including 'the horrible murder of a child by starvation', dreadful executions, foul tortures and one of the earliest mentions of a now notorious killer who turned his victims into pies, this selection of gruesome tales will chill all but the sturdiest of hearts. Many of these tales have not appeared in print since Charles Dickens himself read them. Illustrated with original woodcuts, it will fascinate anyone with an interest in true crime.

Visit our website and discover thousands of other History Press books.
www.thehistorypress.co.uk